COULD YOU BE SUFFERING FROM LATE LIFE DEPRESSION?

TAKE THIS QUIZ

- HAVE YOU LOST FRIENDS OR A SPOUSE AND FEEL THERE'S NO POINT IN LIVING?

- HAVE YOU DROPPED MANY OF YOUR ACTIVITIES AND INTERESTS BECAUSE YOU THINK YOU ARE JUST TOO OLD?

- DO YOU THINK OLDER PEOPLE SLEEP LESS, AND THAT'S WHY YOU'RE HAVING TROUBLE SLEEPING?

- DO YOU FEEL YOU CAN'T TRY NEW THINGS, TRAVEL, OR START A RELATIONSHIP BECAUSE YOU'RE "BEYOND ALL THAT"?

- ARE YOU TOO TIRED TO GO OUT AND OFTEN SIT AROUND THINKING ABOUT THE PAST AND FEELING BLUE?

- DO YOU FEEL THAT "AT YOUR AGE" YOU HAVE NOTHING TO LOOK FORWARD TO EXCEPT DECLINING HEALTH?

YOU *CAN* FEEL GOOD AGAIN.
FIND OUT HOW IN . . .

LATE LIFE DEPRESSION

Also by Patrick Mathiasen
An Ocean of Time: Alzheimer's: Tales of Hope
and Forgetting

Also by Suzanne LeVert
Melatonin: The Anti-Aging Hormone

The Breast Cancer Prevention Program
(with Samuel S. Epstein, M.D)

Out of the Fog: Treatment Options and Coping Strategies
for Adult Attention Deficit Disorder
(with Kevin R. Murphy, Ph.D.)

The Woman Doctor's Guide to Menopause
(with Lois Jovanovic, M.D.)

LATE LIFE DEPRESSION

Patrick Mathiasen, M.D.,
and
Suzanne LeVert

A Dell Book

Published by
Dell Publishing
a division of
Bantam Doubleday Dell Publishing Group, Inc.
1540 Broadway
New York, New York 10036

ISBN: 0-440-22505-1

Printed in the United States of America

Published simultaneously in Canada

January 1998

10 9 8 7 6 5 4 3 2 1

OPM

Authors' Note

In order to preserve privacy interests, the patients portrayed in this book are composites of two or more individuals and do not depict any one individual patient. All names and identities have been altered to protect patients' privacy.

This book is not intended as a substitute for medical advice of mental health professionals. The reader should consult a doctor in matters relating to his or her health and particularly in respect to symptoms that may require diagnosis or medical attention.

In a real dark night of the soul it is always three o'clock in the morning.
—F. Scott Fitzgerald

Contents

Introduction

Depression—a dull, gray force that steadily spreads into the corners and hidden spaces of one's life, its deadly silence forming a shroud over everyday existence. Depression moves ever outward, enveloping friends, spouses, and caregivers in its mist, like a huge gray cloud settling down until all is darkness.

Yet, despite these very apt metaphors, depression is not an intangible outside force, but a physical illness every bit as real as diabetes, heart disease, or cancer. The illness affects both the body and the spirit and in its severe forms may even lead its sufferers to suicide to escape from its pain. It is a disease that can strike at any age, from childhood to late life.

The good news is that treatment for depression exists that can lift the weight of depression. Unfortunately, as people age, the obstacles to successful treatment mount as the disease becomes camouflaged by a number of myths and misconceptions. The first myth is that as we get older, depression is normal: Who wouldn't be depressed, we think, with all the losses—of family and friends, of our physical integrity, of our independence—that come with age? But while grieving our losses is normal, the biological changes that occur with depression require treatment.

Another misconception is that depression is somehow a weakness of character and will. For the elderly in this society, this myth is a particularly difficult one to overcome, since they were taught never to complain, to "pull themselves up by the bootstraps," to take care of their own problems. This leaves them no room to seek or accept help for a medical illness that they cannot conquer on their own.

Finally, there is the view that depression always takes the form of sadness and despondency, that tearfulness and "feeling blue" are its only symptoms. As we age, however, depression can appear in our lives in a number of different guises—nervousness and anxiety, sleeping problems, loss of appetite, and a bewildering array of physical aches and pains that make no sense to their sufferers or their physicians.

The result of these pervasive myths about depression is that although depression is no more common in late life than at any other age, it is far less likely to be recognized and treated. Indeed, doctors often miss depression and thus their older patients suffer needlessly. However, depression is a treatable *medical* illness: More than eighty percent of people who receive treatment feel better. And eighty percent represents a higher success rate than treatment for almost any other condition. State-of-the-art treatments for diabetes, emphysema, and heart disease do not even come close. Furthermore, depression *must be treated,* especially late in life, because it can profoundly affect the physical health of its sufferers. Recent studies show that depression increases the mortality rate—perhaps even doubling it—of those who have heart attacks within the first year after the attack. Indeed, major depression can exacerbate all other medical illnesses, sometimes with lethal effects.

The goal of this book is to help people—those in late life and those who love them—identify the onset of depression and to begin to relieve its symptoms. We devote the first section of the book to understanding depression—what it is, how it appears, how it affects us. The second part examines the various treatments available to treat the disease. And throughout the book we offer case histories of patients to provide you with real-life examples we hope hold meaning for you.

As I write, I think of Mabel: Mabel with the Flowers, as I think of her. Mabel was an eighty-seven-year-old woman, the mother of a close friend, who suffered with a severe depression. But she didn't recognize it as depression.

"I feel like my soul's been invaded!" Mabel said to me when we first met. She went on to describe her life, how it had become devoid of pleasure and all of the good things that she once loved. She didn't understand what had happened, but she knew that something terribly important was missing. She couldn't sleep, she had lost her appetite, and she worried constantly about every little thing.

Mabel stared at me when I told her my diagnosis. "I'm depressed?" she asked. She waved her hands and rolled her eyes. "Come on, now."

It took me the better part of an hour to persuade Mabel to take the antidepressant medications I offered her. And it took even longer to get her to come back and see me. Mabel would never agree to psychotherapy, and she took the medication only with great reluctance.

But Mabel got better, slowly at first, almost imperceptibly. Her energy improved, she began to sleep better, and the smell of food enticed her again. Slowly but surely her world opened up again until one day, four weeks after I began seeing her, she appeared in my office with a bouquet of red roses. "These are for you," she said, pushing them toward me, her smile brightening the room even more than the flowers. Her laughter, as bubbly as champagne, rose up before me. "Thank you," she said. "Thank you for giving me my life back."

As Mabel's experience so clearly showed me, depression is not merely sadness, and it is not a normal side effect of aging. Late life should be a time to look back over one's life, and to look ahead to new challenges. It has the potential to offer as much reward—perhaps even more—than the earlier stages of life. Suzanne and I hope that this book can help you or the loved one you know who suffers from depression to reach out and touch the whole range of life, with all of its ups and downs, its sadnesses and joys.

PART I

Understanding Depression
in Late Life

Depression and aging. For too long we've considered the two conditions to be natural partners. After all, many of the changes that come with age *are* depressing. The toll that time takes on our bodies and our spirits is a heavy one. It's depressing to have to care for a partner who becomes ill. It's hard on the soul to lose loved ones to death and even harder to contemplate our own eventual demise. Yet try as we might to deny it, those changes are very natural and very necessary.

Depression, however, is never a natural condition at any age. It is a serious disease that, in addition to being spiritually and socially demoralizing, often exacerbates or even triggers life-threatening physical illnesses. The fact that most Americans—including many doctors—expect aging and depression to go together keeps the disease hidden and its older victims suffering needlessly. Millions of men and women sixty-five and older—at least 15 percent of this growing population—are unable to enjoy what has become a remarkable time to grow old in America, because of depression.

Indeed, if we look around at our parents and our peers, we see the reality of aging rapidly changing. In any park you can find sixty- and seventy-year-olds walking, jogging, even Rollerblading. Many men and women now work long after the traditional retirement age of sixty-five. More older people than ever before continue to live independently, with their families, or in assisted-living communities. Indeed, most of us now expect to grow older with health and vitality as we strive to help our parents pass through their late lives with grace, dignity, and energy.

Nevertheless, aging remains both inevitable and filled with many psychological, medical, and social challenges. Despite the fact that aging can and should be a vital and satisfying process, we remain a culture rooted in the worship of youth. We're only just now beginning to accept and conceptualize a society in which older people play an integral, natural role. For those entering their "golden years" now, coming to grips with the dichotomy between the vitality that is possible and the continued denigration of old age may be yet another stressful challenge.

No doubt because members of the powerful baby boomer generation are beginning to enter late life in greater numbers every year, attention is now focused on the physical, psychological, and psychosocial issues of late life. In this book we shed some light on the disease of depression, a condition that has for too long remained in the shadows. Part I provides the information you need to know about:

- The social and medical factors that make depression the most common mental health issue of late life
- The signs and symptoms of depression
- The process of diagnosing depression within the often complicated medical and psychosocial context of an older person's life
- The biochemical environment that may make an older

person more vulnerable to depression and what happens in the brain and the body when depression takes hold

Next, Chapter 1 introduces you to the phenomenon of depression, one of the most common medical conditions of the late twentieth century.

CHAPTER ONE

An Age of Melancholy

"I've lived my life, and now I'm just waiting to die," seventy-three-year-old Nick admits. "I guess that's the way it's supposed to be. 'To everything there is a season,' as they say. . . ." The former president of his own construction company, Nick retired three years ago, when arthritis made it difficult to work. In recent months he's required stronger and stronger medicine to quell the pain in his knees and hands, medicine that tires him out and sometimes upsets his stomach. He looks at his future with a sad resignation that deepens day by day, and activities, such as like golf and gardening, that once gave him pleasure now bore him. He feels emotionally disconnected from his family and friends, even from his son and grandchildren, who recently moved nearby to be closer to him.

Seventy-year-old Penny moved with her husband, John, to a residential community in the suburbs two years ago and thought she'd made a satisfying adjustment from city living. At first she found it very lonely because her younger husband, sixty-seven, retained his job on a part-time basis, which kept him far busier—and far more connected to their "old life"—than she. During the last few months, though, she's started to make new friends while volunteering as a mentor to businesswomen in town. Lately, however, stomach problems plague her, and she suffers from headaches her doctor can't explain or resolve. What she hasn't told her doctor is that nightmares about something from her past that she'd hidden from everyone, including herself, for most of her life startle her out of sleep nearly every night.

"Believe it or not, one of my sons just turned nine on the same day I became a grandfather for the first time," sixty-nine-year-old Peter Turner reveals with a sigh. "It's complicated, that much I can tell you. And I know I'm not handling it very well." Peter lives with his second wife, Shannon, a fifty-year-old dress designer for whom this is a first marriage. A business consultant, Peter still keeps his hand in the corporate world, but he is starting to feel tired and anxious about having to maintain such a high energy level. "I thought I knew what it would be like to parent a child at this age, but I was wrong. I want to stop now, smell the roses a little, travel . . . but my wife is deep in her career, Jamie's only nine, and now we're grandparents too. I don't know. I'm overwhelmed."

Janet wakes up at four nearly every morning and cries quietly in the dark until her alarm clock rings three hours later. Despite the fact that she's raised two healthy, loving children and won a battle against alcoholism, sixty-three-year-old Janet spends these hours reflecting on her past with guilt and despair. Now caring for her eighty-three-year-old mother who has a history of bipolar disorder, Janet wonders if these perennial feelings of despondency have to be a permanent part of her own future.

When Julie went to visit her sixty-eight-year-old father, Jake, she found him in a shocking state. "I'd been away for just two weeks, and as soon as I walked into the house, I knew something was terribly wrong," Julie explains. "The shades were drawn, the house was icy cold—I later found out the furnace hadn't been working for at least three days—and dirty dishes and newspapers littered the place. My father was sitting in a chair, just staring. When I asked him a question, he answered in gibberish. The most I could get out of him was a whisper: 'You know, it doesn't matter. It just doesn't matter.' I took him to the doctor right away. I couldn't deny any longer that something was really wrong."

Dianne, a seventy-two-year-old writer, received a diagnosis of early-stage Alzheimer's disease about a year ago. Until quite recently the disease seemed to be progressing very slowly, and Dianne continued to work and socialize as much as ever while experiencing only a few minor memory problems. Lately, however, confusion and despair overwhelm her, especially in the late afternoons. She suffers crying spells over minor setbacks and has begun to forget appointments, friends' names, even events that occurred the day before. "Maybe this is all there is left for me. Maybe this is just the beginning. Some days I can barely pull myself out of bed with the thought of it. I'm alone out here; who will take care of me?"

"Why is this happening to me? Why is God punishing me?" are the questions Maude asks her primary physician. A frail woman of eighty-three, Maude went to her doctor because she had been losing weight and suffering from insomnia, and her medical problems—primarily a heart condition—had been steadily worsening for no apparent reason. Maude's increasing irritability, feelings of desperation, and paranoia are straining her family relationships to the breaking point. It breaks her son Mike's heart to see his mother's last years, which she might spend in relative good health and vitality, being destroyed by an easily treatable but undermining disease like depression.

Seven people—each from a different socioeconomic background, each with a distinct personality, each with a different set of concerns and symptoms, all with at least one thing in common: They suffer from depression, an illness that undermines their sense of self-worth, clouds their hopes for the future, and threatens their health as seriously as any infection or physical disability.

They are not alone. Depression is the most common psychological disorder of late life, affecting at least five million people sixty-five and older. In some groups, such as elders living in nursing homes or the chronically ill, that percentage climbs to 25 percent or higher. Yet the problem of depression in late life often remains a hidden one, masked by other illnesses, shrouded in unnecessary shame, overlooked or dismissed by family, friends, and doctors. Needless suffering is the result, with millions of older men and women struggling alone when treatment—if only sought and applied—could add years of better health to their lives.

At any age depression is one of the most common health problems in the United States today. According to the National Institute of Mental Health, more than 1 in 20 Americans—some 17.8 million people—suffer from depression every year. Depression is an expensive illness, costing the American economy about forty-four billion dollars annually in lost workdays, poor performance on the job, psychotherapeutic care, and loss of lifetime earnings because of suicide. Not included in that figure is the cost of medical care for chronic illnesses and disability so often caused or exacerbated by depression in late life.

As financially burdensome as depression may be, its personal costs are incalculable. It is a disease that robs the spirit of life and the body of energy. Measured by days spent in bed and body pain experienced, depression ranks second only to advanced heart disease in exacting a physical toll. A 1989 study published by the *Journal of the American Medical Association* reported that depression is more isolating and socially debilitating than any other chronic illness. When coupled with the loneliness that so often develops in an elderly person's life, the isolation of depression all too often becomes an unbearable burden. The rate of suicide among people over eighty is up to six times the rate of suicide in teenagers or young adults. Suicide among the elderly is fast becoming a major public health problem.

Depression's impact on the family relationships is often devastating. Someone suffering from depression tends to push away the warm blanket of companionship and intimacy just when it is needed most. Not only does the depressed person suffer from profound loneliness, but family and friends often end up feeling equally isolated and helpless. In fact studies show that more than 40 percent of people living with a depressed person require some psychological help to cope with their own emotional problems. At any age about one in five spouses of a depressed person becomes depressed himself or herself.

Perhaps you've picked up this book because you're concerned that you might be suffering from depression. You feel overwhelmed and afraid, like Peter and Dianne, or sad and mired in self-doubt, like Janet, or you can't quite pinpoint what's causing your stomach upsets or anxiety, like Penny and Maude. Or perhaps, like Jake's daughter, Julie, and Nick's wife, Angela, you've noticed that an older person close to you—a parent, a spouse, a sibling, your adult child—seems more withdrawn, anxious, or disturbed than usual and you're worried about his or her mental health.

If so, you've taken an important step toward coming to grips with a disease that has the potential to rob you or your loved one of precious years. Your step is one that not everyone takes. A panel of experts from the National Institutes of Health warned that more than 60 percent of older Americans suffering from depression do not receive appropriate therapy, often because both health care providers and the affected individuals fail to consider depression a possible cause of persistent sadness, anxiety, or physical symptoms.

The good news is that more than 80 percent of people who do undergo treatment for depression experience a significant improvement within just a few months. In recent decades scientists have developed new medications that effectively alleviate symptoms with very few, and usually very mild, side effects, even among older Americans undergoing treatment for other ailments. Psychotherapeutic techniques are becoming ever more tailored to an individual's personal needs, circumstances, and goals. We discuss these options in depth in later chapters. Whether it's you or someone you love who is depressed, it's important that you understand that you're not alone in what must now seem like a terribly solitary place.

Depression: A Disorder of Modern Times?

As we discuss at some length in Chapter 4, depression is a medical disease that appears to be caused by an imbalance of brain chemicals responsible for transmitting messages about mood and behavior. When these chemicals no longer function efficiently, a number of symptoms may result. These include feelings of sadness and hopelessness; physical changes, such as weight loss, insomnia, and headaches; and cognitive deficits, including memory loss and difficulty with concentration. What causes this imbalance to occur in the first place remains somewhat of a mystery. In some cases, because certain events or circumstances trigger the imbalance, the disorder is known as a reactive depression, while in other cases, known as endogenous depression, symptoms seem to appear out of the blue.

We do know that the late twentieth century seems to offer an especially fertile ground for its development. Depression is the most common mental health disorder in America today, affecting close to 20 percent of the population at some point during their lifetime. The rates of depression among those sixty-five and older have remained relatively steady (about 15 percent), but many scientists believe that members of the baby boomer generation may be even more susceptible to the disease and thus expect this percentage to increase dramatically in years to come. In fact one study found that people born during the 1950s are twenty times more likely to suffer from bouts of depression than those born during the 1920s.

Why are we modern citizens at such risk? No doubt part of the reason for the increase in depression is that the media have helped spread the word about depression and its symptoms, leading more people (and their doctors) to identify the disorder as the cause of physical and mental problems. But that's just a small part of the picture. Many sociologists and psychologists believe that the last several decades of dramatic social change have left modern men and women particularly vulnerable to mood disorders like depression.

Family life is no longer the reliable institution it once was, for instance, and few of us growing older today can count on the kind of emotional support that our parents and grandparents usually received within the family. Religious, moral, and cultural traditions have waned as well, along with our trust in social structures like the government and educational institutions. Cynicism has largely replaced patriotism in the national psyche.

This social disintegration, with its aftereffects of isolation and loneliness, creates ripe ground for depression to take root at any age. As we get older and begin to lose family members and friends to death, however, this disconnectedness leaves us especially vulnerable. In addition, this lack of a sense of community leads many people to feel as if they were struggling only for themselves. Thus their failures (even the minor ones) may devastate them while their successes (even the major ones) seem hollow, especially, perhaps, when examined in retrospect as they approach the last stage of life. "I lived, I had some children, and now, or pretty soon anyway, I'll die," Janet reflects. "I wonder, what's the point? What did it mean? Why should I bother to keep up this struggle? I look at my mother, twenty years older than I am and still struggling. It defeats me."

As we discuss further in Chapter 6, one of the goals of psychotherapy for depressed older men and women is to help them put their lives into perspective with more clarity and objectivity, if not optimism; to be able to tell themselves the stories of their lives with a measure of grace and pride. For now, it's important to remember that the disease of depression is never a "normal" response to aging or even to the slow process of accepting our own mortality. We may feel sad, angry, even worthless at times as we struggle with getting older, but the symptoms of depression are far more profound than those feelings. Indeed depression is a disease every bit as real and debilitating as diabetes and arthritis.

Who gets depressed?

Depression does not discriminate. The disorder affects people of every age, race, religion, and culture. It is neither an inevitable side effect of aging nor a disorder reserved for the young and stereotypically self-indulgent. In fact, each of us is more or less vulnerable to the disease depending on a variety of factors. Among the factors that raise one's general risk are family history of depression, gender, and age.

The family connection: Like many other physical and psychological disorders, depression has a genetic component, which means that it tends to run in families. Janet, for instance, may have inherited a predisposition for mood disorders from her mother, who herself suffers with bipolar disorder and who had an uncle and a grandparent with depression. Although researchers have yet to identify the specific genes involved, studies show that relatives of people with depression have an overall two to three times higher risk of developing the disease than people without family histories of the disease. A child with one depressed parent has a 26 percent higher risk, while one with two depressed parents carries a 46 percent higher risk.

The genetic connection is strongest between identical twins brought up together in the same family. If one identical twin becomes depressed, the other runs about a 76 percent chance of developing the disorder. Even if the twins are raised separately, the concordance rate—the rate of similarity—is about 67 percent. This statistic points to the strong genetic component involved in the development of depression.

If your parents suffered with depression, does this mean that you are doomed to suffer too? Not necessarily. It only means that your *risk* of depression is higher than someone without a family history. Clearly, environmental, psychological, and physical factors, such as the way you've been brought up, the stresses you face day to day, and your physiological makeup, also come into play when it comes to a complex disorder like depression. But if you understand your family's genetic vulnerability and watch carefully for early signs of depression, you may be able to get help before a depressive disorder takes hold.

"All my life, I've known my risks were higher than others' for becoming depressed," Janet admits, "and once I had my first bout, at about twenty-five, I really tried to stay alert to the warning signs. Mine always started with wanting to be in bed more than anything else and overeating. If I notice I'm starting to do those things, I try to see my therapist right away. Unfortunately sometimes the disease overtakes my motivation, and I slip under anyway. Like now."

The good news for some, however, is that it appears that the later in life depression occurs for the first time, the weaker the genetic connection. Jake's depression, triggered in part by the death of his wife, is his first experience with mental illness. "As far as I know," his daughter, Julie, reports, "his side of the family all lived to a ripe old age without a hint of emotional problems. My dad's depression seemed to come from out of the blue. Maybe that's why it's so scary. I wonder if I should worry as I get older too."

Julie probably has less to worry about than children of parents whose first bouts of depression struck much earlier in life. Studies show that the risk for immediate relatives of patients with depression that occurred later than age fifty to be about 8.3 percent, compared with about 26 percent for relatives of patients who had onset before the age of fifty.

The gender gap: Depression appears to be one of the most gender-specific of all psychological disorders. At every age women are two to three times more likely than men to develop a depressive mood disorder. According to the *Diagnostic and Statistical Manual of Mental Disorders (DSM-IV)*, the American Psychiatric Association's guidebook, a woman's lifetime risk for major depression ranges from 10 to 25 percent, compared with 5 to 12 percent for men.

Both psychosocial and biological reasons help explain this gender difference in depression rates. Older women, in particular, face special challenges that may help trigger depression: According to recent statistics, a woman who reaches the age of sixty-five in relatively good health is likely to live until eighty-five or older. More than likely, though, she will live these years alone; of the nine million people over sixty-five living alone today, nearly 80 percent of them are women. Some never married, others have lost their spouses to death or divorce, but the end result is that they have to fend for themselves for perhaps another two decades. Such a situation creates both financial and emotional stress, especially as illness and disability take hold, and stress, as we see later, often lays the groundwork for depression.

"Part of the reason I'm so upset," admits Dianne, "is that I'm alone. I've always been an independent woman and never wanted to be married. But getting old, getting sick were such abstract concepts for me that I never made a plan. Now that I see a long road of illness ahead, I'm terribly worried."

Another heavy burden for women is their frequent role as caregivers to their parents, siblings, spouses, and children. More than 72 percent of all caregivers are women, who spend an average of eighteen years caring for their spouses or parents in late life. The average age of caregivers is fifty-seven, but 25 percent of caregivers are between the ages of sixty-five and seventy-five and another 10 percent are seventy-five years and older. The burdens of caregiving are myriad (we discuss these challenges in greater length in Chapter 8) and frequently trigger depression and other illnesses in the women who take on such responsibilities. According to the Family Caregivers Alliance, about 49 percent of female caregivers develop depression, and caregivers are two to three times more likely to use prescription drugs for depression, anxiety, and insomnia than the general population.

Most researchers believe that a woman's physiology, so closely regulated by hormonal fluctuations, is a prime reason for depression's apparent gender gap. Without question, such biological events as monthly menstruation, giving birth, and the onset of menopause often trigger depression in women. As we explain further in Chapter 4, the female hormone estrogen exerts a powerful influence on certain brain chemicals called neurotransmitters that have been linked closely with depression.

Another consideration is the different coping skills women learn as they grow up in this gender-based society. Many psychologists believe that men and women are raised to respond differently to the same stimuli: Men learn to be more aggressive and to express their anger better than women. Women tend to react rather than to act and to focus more than men do on relationships with others as a source of happiness and self-esteem. Women are also more likely to turn the blame inward and punish themselves, while men tend to respond to frustration and disappointment by acting with violence or succumbing to substance abuse.

Furthermore, violence in this society is perpetrated too often by men against women and too often by men presumed to love the women they abuse. According to statistics compiled by the Federal Bureau of Investigation, a woman is battered every fifteen seconds by an intimate partner. Sexual abuse is just as common. The American Psychological Association Special Task Force on Women and Depression revealed that a shocking 37 percent of women have a significant experience of physical or sexual abuse before the age of twenty-one.

Each woman who suffers this kind of victimization runs a higher risk of developing depression, both while enduring the abuse and later, as a symptom of posttraumatic stress disorder. Penny, for instance, is just learning that her current struggle with depression and panic stems from sexual abuse she received at the hands of her grandfather more than sixty years ago. The entire female sex may be affected by this widespread violence and abuse. Even if they escape being victims themselves, most women may feel less secure, less able to trust their instincts, less in control of their destinies—at least in terms of violence—than their male counterparts and thus perhaps more susceptible to mood disorders like depression.

At the same time, however, the gender gap of depression may not be as wide as current statistics indicate. Research shows that a similar pattern of chemical imbalances that occur with depression also occurs in people who commit violence or become addicted to alcohol or drugs—specifically a disruption in the level of a neurotransmitter called serotonin. That means that stress causes very similar changes in brain chemistry in both men and women, but they react differently to these changes on the basis of the way they've been brought up.

This would help explain why rates for both violence among men and depression among women have steadily climbed, apparently in tandem, during the late twentieth century. It may also explain the difference in suicide rates between men and women. At all ages men are three times as likely to commit suicide as women (usually with firearms), but women attempt suicide and fail much more frequently than men (probably because they use less violent and more reversible means, like ingesting overdoses of pills). Homicides are a particularly male phenomenon as well, with men making up the majority of both victims and perpetrators of deadly violent acts.

Could it be that men are just as depressed as women but express it in very different ways? A 1997 book by psychotherapist Terrence Real, aptly titled *I Don't Want to Talk About It,* postulates that many men may suffer from what he calls covert depression. In this view, violence, substance abuse, and anger may be the most common symptoms of depression for men, while women experience the more typical symptoms of sadness and hopelessness. If this theory holds true, and both men and their doctors learn to recognize the signs of depression, millions of men may finally receive the help they need to resolve their internal pain.

The age factor: Depression recognizes no age barrier. Children, teenagers, and adults of all ages develop depression. Depression does not bypass the so-called carefree days of youth or represent an inevitable consequence of aging, like graying hair and wrinkling skin. Each age group has its own separate stressors that put its members at risk.

For the most part, depression tends to spare young children, with only about 1 percent succumbing to the disorder. As children enter puberty, however, more and more of them become depressed. About 5 percent of adolescents develop major depression, and an additional 3.5 percent suffer from chronic mild depression (dysthymia). Unfortunately depression in adolescents is often masked by other problems, ranging from learning disabilities to eating disorders to substance abuse. Depression in this age group can be lethal if left untreated: Approximately five thousand adolescents kill themselves in the United States each year, and another four hundred thousand make unsuccessful attempts. Today suicide represents the third leading cause of death in adolescents.

The most common age group for depression is between twenty and forty-four. About one in four women and one in ten men will develop depression during this period. The average age when a person experiences his or her first bout of depression is between twenty and twenty-two, about ten years earlier than in the 1950s and 1960s. Today about 10 percent of young adults will have already experienced at least one bout of depression by age twenty-five. After age forty-four or so, depression rates tend to level off until late in life.

As discussed, old age does not mean automatic melancholy. Just the opposite is true; relatively healthy, independent men and women over the age of sixty-five experience slightly less depression, on average, than younger adults. About 15 percent of the general population over sixty-five is depressed in any given year, with as many as 25 to 30 percent of nursing home residents suffering from the disease, probably because of the combination of increased isolation and severe illness they experience. The chronically ill—and those family members or spouses who care for them—also have high rates of depression.

As we show in the chapters that follow, many factors complicate the diagnosis and treatment of depression in late life. Some illnesses common among the elderly, such as heart disease, and chronic conditions, like arthritis and Alzheimer's disease, can trigger depression while masking its symptoms. When physical disorders are also present, a diagnosis of depression can be difficult to make and may easily be overlooked.

RISK FACTORS FOR DEPRESSION IN LATE LIFE

- Having a personal or family history of depression
- Being female
- Having a chronic illness or caring for someone who does
- Suffering the loss of a spouse
- Lacking a social support system
- Abusing alcohol or drugs

Perhaps the greatest stumbling block to overcome in terms of recognizing late life depression is a subtle "ageism" among doctors, family members, and even the elderly themselves. Like Nick, the seventy-three-year-old man you met at the beginning of the chapter, we all tend to be too quick to attribute depressive symptoms to medical problems or as a natural, expected side effect of aging.

"Even my neighbor said that maybe my 'bad mood' was an appropriate response to the fact that I'm getting older, that I have a chronic illness, and that my life is almost finished," Nick remarks. "I guess we all kind of expect old people to be sad and depressed. I'm finding out, though, that there's no need for me to feel this way."

When the Golden Years Are Not So Golden

To reiterate: Depression is *not* a natural part of aging, nor should any older person assume that a medical disease is necessarily responsible for depressive symptoms. Keep in mind that the vast majority of older people face the challenges of age without experiencing depression or other mental health problems. That said, there are certain physical, medical, social, and emotional changes that take place as we age, changes that may leave us more vulnerable to disease. Indeed, although advances in medical science now allow more and more people to live longer, there is no guarantee that these extra years will be healthy, happy, or rewarding. Some of the challenges faced by men and women entering late life include:

Coping with physical changes: The biology of aging is a fascinating branch of science, and every day we learn more about how and why the human body ages. For the most part, the news is good. Getting older does not mean an automatic and relentless sinking into illness. In fact aging appears to be a uniquely individual process, with each person undergoing changes at different times and in different ways. One man may have a massive heart attack at sixty-five, recover, and go on to live a vital and healthy life until he develops a fatal cancer in his eighties. Another man, experiencing the same type of heart attack at the same age, may quickly succumb to chronic illness and disability and spend a few final years practically bedridden.

Some of our fate lies in heredity (the ages at which your parents and grandparents died may give you a clue to your own potential life span, for instance), but much of it is under our control. Evidence continues to accumulate that continued physical exercise and mental stimulation are the best antidotes to aging; the adage "Use it or lose it" proves remarkably accurate when it comes to keeping our minds and bodies fit as we get older.

THE TRUTH ABOUT AGING

Answer these questions true or false; then check at the end of the chapter to see how influenced you are by stereotypes about aging.

1. Everyone becomes confused or forgetful if he or she lives long enough.
   True   *False*

2. The older you get, the less you sleep.
   True   *False*

3. Most older people are depressed.
   True   *False*

4. Older people can't take medication for depression because they take too many other drugs.
   True   *False*

5. People begin to lose interest in sex at around age fifty-five.
   True   *False*

6. If one of your parents had Alzheimer's disease, you're doomed to get it too.
   True   *False*

7. As your body changes with age, so does your personality.
   True   *False*

8. You can be too old to exercise.
   True   *False*

9. Suicide is mainly a problem for teenagers.
   True   *False*

10. You can't teach an old dog new tricks.
    True   *False*

On the other hand, aging is without question an inevitable process. Sooner or later our skin will wrinkle, our hair will lose color and turn gray, our bones and muscles will weaken, and our immune systems will no longer be able to fight as hard against infection or the steady deterioration of our internal organ systems. Our senses become muted: our taste buds less sharp, our hearing and sight less acute. Fortunately brain function remains intact for most of us, with only subtle—often barely unnoticeable—changes taking place in the ability to retrieve words or memories quickly.

Coming to terms with these changes is a challenge for most men and women, especially since our culture remains deeply rooted in the myth that "youth equals beauty." Depending on the presence and severity of chronic illness, these physical changes may feel overwhelming.

Facing loss: Although more and more people find late life a time of opportunity, a stage of life offering freedom to explore new horizons, this freedom usually does not come without a price. Some have more time since, like Nick, they no longer can work because of illness or disability. Others have been forced to retire by a working America that continues to favor brawn and youth over wisdom and experience.

Although some women see life after menopause as a time to enjoy sexuality free of worries about pregnancy, others find that the loss of fertility undermines their sense of self. That children have left the nest usually means more privacy, time, and money, but it also can mean loneliness and disconnection from important social contact with younger generations. Sometimes a couple's move from a now too large, too expensive house to a more efficient apartment results not only in a release from a financial and physical burden but also in the loss of continuity, history, and sense of place. As these and other types of loss mount, so too does the stress. Add to this the loss of loved ones to death and disease, and you have ripe ground for depression in vulnerable individuals.

For some men and women entering late life, the sense of loss comes from another place altogether: from the loss of what "old" was supposed to mean. "It's hard to describe really, and I keep hoping that I'll work through it because I love my son and my wife very much," Peter Turner says, "but I think I'm grieving about the life of retirement I grew up believing I'd have, one that I rejected completely ten years ago, when I decided to have a child at a time when my youngest daughter from my previous marriage was already twenty-five years old and planning her wedding. I know it sounds terribly selfish, but I'm wondering now if there will ever be a time for me, a time of my own."

Surviving bereavement: "Old age is an island surrounded by death" was the rather grim pronouncement made by the nineteenth-century Ecuadoran philosopher and political leader Juan Montalvo. While the births of grandchildren and great-grandchildren provide many older men and women with a sustaining link to the future, an inevitable consequence of life is coping with death. In the average year more than two million people die, the vast majority of them over the age of sixty-five, leaving about eight million family members—one million of them spouses—and millions more friends, former schoolmates, and peers to grieve.

"It was awful for my father when my mother died a few years ago," Julie says. "But it wasn't only her death; it was the death of other people he knew: old army buddies, people from the old neighborhood he hadn't seen for years. It was more the *mounting* losses, the 'tally,' so to speak, that really upset him.''

As we discuss further in Chapter 3, grief itself, even the deep grief that almost suffocates with its intensity, is not depression. Scientists believe, however, that bereavement can set in motion the biochemical and emotional cycle that allows depression to take hold, and until the depression is treated, the process of grieving may not proceed in a natural fashion.

Remaining independent: Without question, retaining financial and personal independence is the number-one goal for men and women growing older, and the fear of losing it is one of the most pervasive and undermining anxieties of middle and late life. ''I've lived on my own or with my husband all my life,'' eighty-three-year-old Maude explains. ''And when he died three years ago, I started to get really scared. I don't want to be a burden to my children, and I don't want to go into a home. I've got some money, but it might not be enough. I don't know what will happen to me.''

Maude's experience is fairly typical for the generation that came into late life during the 1980s and 1990s, in that most people remained financially independent and remarkably healthy compared with their ancestors. Thanks largely to the social programs like Medicaid, put into place during the Johnson administration, the poverty rate among the elderly fell from an average of 32 percent in the 1960s to 12 percent today, and the proportion of seniors moving into nursing homes—once an expected but dreaded consequence of aging—has fallen steadily during the past few decades. According to the National Center for

Health Statistics, fewer than 5 percent of Americans over the age of sixty-five now live in nursing homes, down 18 percent since 1985. Even of those over eighty-five, just one in four now lives in a nursing home.

Nevertheless, the specter of fear about losing one's financial or physical independence is pervasive. How many times have you heard your parents say, or said yourself, "I'd rather die than go into a home," or "Pull the plug if I ever become incapacitated"? As we get older, these worries can become distressing, even incapacitating anxieties.

Avoiding isolation: One of the single greatest risk factors for depression in late life is a lack of social support and interaction. In fact recent research shows that social isolation is a risk factor for the development of diseases of any kind. According to a study at Harvard University, for instance, loneliness is a more important influence than high cholesterol in the development of heart disease, and a team of scientists at the University of California found that group support formed a crucial part of cancer treatment.

"I'm so thankful for my friends," Dianne remarks. "They are my family. I don't have anyone but good friends and a few nieces and nephews. I've always worked alone. I've got enough money, but now I look back and wonder. . . . Jean Rostand, a favorite writer of mine, once wrote, 'To be an adult is to be alone.' That's never had more meaning to me than it does today." As we discuss in Chapters 7 and 8, establishing a supportive social network is a key ingredient in both the treatment of depression and the prevention of relapses.

Managing   interpersonal   relationships: The flip side of isolation and its dangers to mental and physical health is the stress that sustaining relationships often involves. Indeed one of the greatest challenges we face as we grow older is coping with the sheer complexity of our personal relationships. Just by living this long, we have created a network of interrelated friends, lovers, family members, acquaintances. The history and dynamics of those relationships deeply affect how we relate to the people around us today. Moreover, the demands made upon us by others often interfere with the establishment of new relationships or the vitality of long-term partnerships.

"At first, it wasn't so hard to meld my new wife into my existing circle of friends and family," Peter explains. "We had enough mutual interests that my older and her younger friends had some common ground. But now I'm worried about whether to send my kid to private high school in a few years while my peers are deciding if they should move to a resort community somewhere down South. And now I'm a grandfather to a beautiful little girl, and believe it or not, my son's jealous. I'm dealing with sibling rivalry between generations. What did I get myself into? I wonder sometimes how to make my life work within this complex of people and priorities."

He isn't alone. More than 50 percent of couples over sixty-five are members of four generations, and about 20 percent of women over eighty (the fastest-growing segment of the population) are great-great-grandmothers, matriarchs of five generations. That means that today's grandparent is likely to be a grandson or granddaughter as well as a spouse, sibling, aunt or uncle, and friend to a myriad of people of all ages. According to "The Age Boom" in the March 10, 1997, *New York Times,* despite the fact that most families have two working parents, grandparents are raising approximately 3.5 million children, and 6 million families depend on grandparents for primary child care.

Balancing those roles without neglecting ourselves or the needs of loved ones is one of the greatest challenges we face today. In spite of these challenges—or maybe even because of them—late life provides most of its residents a haven for reflection and an avenue for exploration. For those who become depressed, however, this time of life can become one of brutal chronic illness and isolation.

Depression Makes It Worse

Perhaps depression's most dangerous side effect is its ability to sap from its victims the will to live, to enjoy, to care what happens today, to have hope for the future. In older individuals, especially those who suffer from other illnesses, such an effect can lead to a host of serious problems. In fact depression can make almost any illness or disability worse. Without treatment, depression can all too often lead to:

- Increased disability
- Intensified pain and other medical symptoms
- Heightened sensitivity to the side effects of many medications
- Cognitive impairment

- Substance abuse
- Anorexia (dramatic loss of appetite)
- Neglect of necessary medical care and self-care
- Increased hospitalization and prolonged rehabilitation
- Suicide

As you can see, it is urgent that an older person suffering from depression receive treatment before the disease has a chance to further undermine health. In the vast majority of cases, medication and/or therapy will return the body and mind to their former state of balance and health. Before that can happen, however, the symptoms of depression must be recognized and brought to the attention of a mental health professional. In Chapter 2 we describe those symptoms and how they may present themselves in an older person. You'll be better able to evaluate your own symptoms or those of an older person in your life.

Important Questions and Answers About Chapter 1

Q. I know that rates of depression are different between men and women. What about single and married people? Are they equally vulnerable?

A. There does appear to be a correlation between marital state and depression. A University of California study of seven thousand American adults showed that men between the ages of forty-five and sixty-four with wives were twice as likely to live ten years longer than their single counterparts. Men without women are twice as likely to suffer from depression as married men, and widowed men are also likely to suffer marked deterioration after the death of their wives.

Q. My father was recently diagnosed with depression. He also has high blood pressure. Should I be afraid of a heart attack?

A. You're right to be concerned. Scientists believe that depression plays an important role in the development or course of a host of serious and chronic conditions, including heart disease. A 1996 study at Johns Hopkins University followed two thousand Baltimore men and women for more than thirteen years. It found that 8 percent of those who suffered severe depression and 6 percent of those who had experienced milder depression later had heart attacks. Among those with no histories of depression, only 3 percent suffered heart attacks. When the findings were adjusted for age, gender, smoking, and medical histories, the gap widened: Those who had had major depressions were four times more likely to have heart attacks than those who had never been depressed.

Q. Are symptoms of depression in older people different from those in younger people?

A. Generally no. However, many older men and women experience depression within a complicated medical picture, in which medication or other illnesses can mask or exacerbate their depression. In addition, older people tend to resist more firmly the idea that a mental illness could be causing their problems. For these reasons their primary symptoms tend to be somatic ones, like headaches and gastrointestinal disturbances. In Chapter 2, we outline the many different forms depression may take and describe its symptoms in more depth.

Now for the answers to the "Truth About Aging" quiz on pages 23–24.

1. *False.* Neither confusion nor significant memory loss is normal at any age, and it should be evaluated by a health professional as soon as possible.
2. *False.* In later life it's the quality of sleep, not the total sleep time, that declines. (In Chapter 4 we explain the connection between sleep and depression, then in Chapter 10 discuss how to get a better night's sleep.)
3. *False.* Most older people are not depressed, and depression is no more a "normal" side effect of aging than is heart disease or cancer. Furthermore, doctors can treat depression no matter when it occurs in the life cycle by using a variety of approaches, such as psychotherapy and family support and medication. (We outline treatment options in Part II.)
4. *False.* Although it's true that older people often suffer with a number of conditions requiring medication, including heart disease, hypertension, and diabetes, their doctors can usually find safe and effective antidepressants for them. However, it's extremely important to receive careful medical care should you have depression that requires medication. (We describe the medications available to treat depression and provide a list of adverse effects and contraindications in Chapter 5.)
5. *False.* Most older people can—and do—experience healthy, satisfying sex lives. However,

sexual dysfunction may occur because of depression or, ironically, because of medications you're taking to treat depression. (We talk about the way depression affects intimate relationships in Chapter 8 and medication-related sexual problems in Chapter 6.)

6. *False.* The overwhelming majority of people with Alzheimer's disease *do not* have family histories of the disease. Furthermore, even if Alzheimer's runs in your family, do not assume that memory problems or confusion automatically means dementia. In fact confusion and forgetfulness are often the first signs of depression in older people. (In Chapter 3 we provide you with more information about the differences between dementia and depression.)

7. *False.* Unless someone suffers from a neurological disorder like Alzheimer's disease or another form of dementia, aging does not affect the parts of the brain responsible for personality. If you or someone you love begins to act out of character, it may be appropriate to see a physician for an evaluation.

8. *False.* Exercise at any age can help strengthen the heart and lungs, lower blood pressure, and elevate mood. It can especially help alleviate depression. (We explain the physiology of exercise and provide tips for older people to begin and maintain safe exercise programs in Chapter 8.)

9. *False.* Suicide rates are highest among white men over the age of eighty-five, and they are just as high as teenage rates in white men from

age sixty-five and up. An older person's preoccupation with suicide should be taken seriously, and professional help should be sought quickly. We discuss suicide and suicide prevention in more depth in Chapter 4.

10. *False.* At any age people can learn new information and skills. Pablo Casals, the world-class cellist who performed concerts well into his eighties, put it this way: "Age is a relative matter. If you continue to work and absorb the beauty of the world around you, you find that age doesn't necessarily mean getting old."

CHAPTER TWO

Recognizing Depression's Signs and Symptoms

In *Darkness Visible,* William Styron's moving account of his descent into depression at the age of sixty, the author finds "depression" too bland, too sluggish a word to describe the deep agitation, confusion, and despair that plagued him. Styron agrees with the nineteenth-century writer and fellow depression sufferer William James that depression is not a repression of feeling, as the word might imply, but rather something far more organic and alive. "It is a positive and active anguish," James wrote, "a sort of psychical neuralgia wholly unknown to normal life." In the end Styron offers the word "brainstorm" as a potential alternative, because of the "howling tempest" of symptoms that occur in this disease, but he remains dissatisfied.

Even these men, whose remarkable powers of description are evident in their life's work, couldn't find the right words to describe the way depression felt to them. To add to the challenge, it appears that each person who suffers from depression experiences it in a different way, in a different rhythm and pattern. In a moment you'll read about the way depression feels to the seven people you met in the first chapter. First, try to answer the following questions as openly and honestly as you can, then read on to find out what your answers may mean to your health.

Are you basically satisfied with your life?	Yes	*No*
Have you dropped many of your activities and interests?	*Yes*	No
Do you feel that your life is empty?	*Yes*	No
Do you often get bored?	*Yes*	No
Are you in good spirits most of the time?	Yes	*No*
Are you afraid something bad is going to happen to you?	*Yes*	No
Do you feel happy most of the time?	Yes	*No*
Do you often feel helpless?	*Yes*	No
Do you prefer to stay at home rather than go out and do new things?	*Yes*	No
Do you think you have more memory problems than most?	*Yes*	No
Do you think it's wonderful to be alive now?	Yes	*No*
Do you feel pretty worthless the way you are now?	*Yes*	No
Do you feel full of energy?	Yes	*No*
Do you think that your situation is hopeless?	*Yes*	No
Do you think that most people are better off than you are?	*Yes*	No

Hopelessness, weariness, dissatisfaction, unworthiness—these are some of the most common and pervasive feelings associated with depression in late life. Do you have these feelings about yourself and your life? If you circled five or more italicized answers that indicate negative feelings, you may well be suffering from depression, depression that requires treatment. No matter what your score, if you think you might be depressed, see your doctor as soon as possible to discuss your concerns.

Remember, if you do suffer from depression, you're not alone, even if it seems that no one else in the world could be feeling the way you do now. In a way, though, you may be right: No one does feel *exactly* the way you do, for again, everyone experiences depression in a unique way.

"Like something came in and sapped the energy right out of me," Nick says when asked to describe the effects of depression. Maude finds herself becoming agitated, yet strangely paralyzed. "I just can't stand to be in my own skin," she admits. "I'm terrible. I'm a terrible person, and I'm being punished. God is punishing me." When Janet suffers an episode of depression, she identifies hopelessness as the pervading emotion. "I've thought about it a lot during the past forty years. I finally hit upon a metaphor I like to use whenever someone asks me what depression feels like. I say it's as if heavy dark draperies drop down and block out all sunlight, all joy, all amusement. It's just dark and too quiet. And sad." "For me," Peter says, "depression has been like a paralysis. I can't move the way I used to, not only emotionally but physically. I feel hunched over, slow . . . old. Scared."

The faces of depression in late life are even more

varied when other mental or physical disorders complicate the situation. Penny also suffers from an accompanying anxiety disorder that leaves her tense and distracted, for instance, while Dianne contends with the creeping memory losses that she fears may have more to do with Alzheimer's disease than with depression. Jake's breakdown is complicated by an underlying grief over his wife's recent death, a grief that he has not resolved in a normal fashion.

Clearly, defining depression is not an easy task, especially when it occurs in older men and women who may be suffering from physical illnesses and/or taking medications that might hide underlying mood disorders. At any age depression is highly variable, affecting everyone who has it in a slightly different way. In fact it may be easier to describe what depression is *not* than what it is. It is not a case of the blues that lasts for a few hours or days. It is not the sadness one feels after a relationship breaks up or the dip in self-esteem and disorientation that comes from failing to meet a goal or facing a disappointment. It is not grief or a bad mood or even feeling consistently grouchy or out of sorts. Instead depression is a pervasive illness that can cause a variety of physical and emotional symptoms. These can be divided into three four distinct categories: somatic disturbances, emotional changes, cognitive symptoms, and behavioral changes.

It's important to be aware that in older people especially, the "typical" symptoms of depression—crying, low moods, feelings of despair—may not be the ones the depressed person first acknowledges or even experiences. The most common first symptoms of depression at any age are frequently not the emotional ones at all but physical, or somatic, ones.

Somatic disturbances

Headaches, stomach problems, insomnia, loss of appetite: The list of physical complaints related to depression is extensive and is often overlooked as possible symptoms of a psychological disorder. In fact most people with depression first visit a doctor, complaining not of emotional problems but of physical ones, and that's particularly true for older Americans, who not only may be suffering from physical illnesses that could account for their symptoms but also may be reticent to discuss emotional problems with their physicians. In Chapter 3 we explain in more depth the difficulty physicians often have in making an accurate diagnosis of depression in an older individual. In the meantime here are the most frequent symptoms of the disorder.

TYPICAL SYMPTOMS OF DEPRESSION

Emotional disturbances
     Crying
     Hopelessness
     Guilt
     Despair
Behavioral changes
     Anorexia (dramatic loss of appetite)
     Social withdrawal
     Loss of interest in activities
     Increase in alcohol use or abuse

Somatic complaints
    Pain
    Headaches
    Decreased energy
    Stomach problems
    Insomnia or hypersomnia
    Loss of appetite or increase in appetite
    Loss of sex drive

ATYPICAL SYMPTOMS OF DEPRESSION

Confusion
Memory loss
Paranoia
Anxiety
Obsessions and compulsions
Unusual behaviors
    Shoplifting
    Sexual promiscuity
    Screaming
Accidental overdoses
Weight gain
Incontinence
Marital discord

Pain: Back pain, headaches, neck pain, pain that can't be defined or located: Perhaps more than any other single somatic complaint, pain is the one that more older people with undiagnosed depression first bring to the attention of their physicians. That was the certainly the case for Penny, whose afternoon headaches and stomachaches nearly crippled her. ''Actually I went back and forth between thinking I had a brain aneurysm or stomach cancer," Penny admits with a laugh. "I think I was so afraid of locating my pain where it really existed—in my heart and soul—that I transferred it to other parts of the body." Unfortunately doctors often prescribe medication in an effort to treat pain when depression is really the problem; paradoxically and tragically the medication tends only to worsen the mood disorder.

Fatigue: Other common and early signs of depression in older people are loss of energy and chronic fatigue. To the outside world, and even to older men and women themselves, this symptom may appear to be merely a "slowing down" that naturally comes with age. Another tendency is to relate the fatigue to a physical illness, such as anemia, arthritis, diabetes, thyroid problems, and infections.

"At first I just thought it was Nick's arthritis that was keeping him away from the golf course," Angela, Nick's wife of forty-five years, remarks. "And I even suspected a hearing loss might account for his distance and isolation at family gatherings. I fell into the trap so many of us do: I just didn't want to think that Nick could be depressed. And I know it was the farthest thing from his mind—well, his conscious mind anyway."

Insomnia: Another common symptom of depression is a change in sleep patterns. Most people with depression suffer from the inability to fall asleep or stay asleep or from early wakening (awakening several hours earlier than normal). "That's the worst part of my depression, this waking up early," Janet says. "Everything looks so dark and bleak at four-thirty in the morning. Sometimes by afternoon I feel better, and so I go to bed thinking maybe it's over, that I'll wake up refreshed and ready to go. Then my eyes snap wide open in the middle of the night, and the descent begins all over again.''

These three forms of insomnia are typical signs of depression in people of all ages. However, like fatigue, insomnia is often seen as a normal side effect of aging. It is true that as we get older, our sleep patterns do change, often leading to difficulty getting and staying asleep. Some scientists believe this change in sleep patterns is due to the age-related loss of certain hormones—namely, melatonin, a hormone produced by the pineal gland in the brain. As we'll see in Chapter 4, excessively low levels of melatonin have been found in depressed people of all ages, further implicating the endocrine system in many cases of mood disorders.

Gastrointestinal disturbances: It's a connection we're all pretty used to: the link between the emotions and the stomach. When we're nervous, we feel "butterflies"; when we're tense, a "knot." Many people who later receive diagnoses of depression arrive at their doctor's office complaining of stomach and intestinal problems, including constipation, diarrhea, and chronic stomachaches. In fact an estimated 70 to 90 percent of people who seek medical care for irritable bowel syndrome—a common gastrointestinal disorder characterized by loose and frequent stools—also have psychiatric problems, usually major depression.

Changes in eating habits: Changes in eating habits also occur in severe depression. In most cases depressed people lose their appetites and hence begin to lose weight. Among the elderly in nursing homes anorexia—an eating disorder marked by profound lack of appetite that can lead to serious health issues—is a significant and often fatal problem. Many mental health professionals suspect that many of the anorexic elderly are suffering from concurrent and undiagnosed depression.

"It wasn't that I didn't want to eat," Jake explains. "I just couldn't care enough about eating to buy the food or cook it. When I did manage to make myself a meal, I wouldn't taste the food. It was just there. Eventually I figured, Why bother at all?"

Please note, however, that many elderly people fail to eat properly for a number of reasons unrelated to depression, including undiscovered illnesses, reactions to medications, decaying teeth or poorly fitting dentures, and even lack of money for food. As you can imagine, not being able to eat or enjoy food is apt to be an incredibly frustrating, humiliating, and distressing side effect of aging, one that by itself could trigger an underlying depression. As we stress in Chapters 7 and 8, making sure that you and the older people in your life receive adequate attention to *all* their needs—not just the obvious medical ones—is crucial if the aging process is to proceed smoothly.

Although loss of appetite is the most common eating-related symptom of depression, many people who become depressed develop the opposite problem: They tend to overeat and gain weight, in effect turning to food for comfort and solace. Penny, for instance, who feels very anxious as well as depressed, finds herself snacking constantly. "I don't even taste what I'm eating, and I certainly don't enjoy the food, but I can't stop," she explains. "So now, on top of everything else, I feel like such a failure for having gained all this weight. I feel out of control."

Loss of libido: "Sex? I haven't even thought about sex in weeks," Peter admits. "I love my wife, and I know it's distressing to her because we've always had an active sex life. I'm not saying we haven't slowed down some as I've gotten older, but I think what convinced me that something really might be going on with me psychologically is this lack of sex drive. It just doesn't feel right, and it's affecting my marriage."

Loss of libido is a frequent side effect of depression, linked to both the biochemical changes that take place in the brain and to the low self-esteem and energy that often accompany a bout with the disorder. Like other somatic symptoms of a mood disorder, loss of libido can also have root causes in several different illnesses and medications. Ironically, certain antidepressants may cause a reduction in sex drive among men and women undergoing treatment for depression.

Furthermore, this symptom—perhaps more than any other—often remains hidden from doctors because of the difficulty many people have in discussing sexual matters. It is also true that many older people simply assume that their sexuality and sexual desire should decrease as they age. Happily, however, research shows that the desire and the ability to enjoy sex do not diminish with age, although its frequency and intensity often do.

"Before Nick got sick, our sex life was better than ever," his wife, Angela, explains. "Instead of being so . . . urgent and hurried, we now took the time to really explore each other. It was more about nurturing and comfort than anything else. I want to get that back."

Emotional changes

Perhaps the most obvious impact depression has is on our feelings and our moods. Sadness is the most common feeling, and tearfulness its frequent expression. "Mornings have always been the most difficult for me," Janet admits, "but the truth is, I find myself crying at the oddest times. All of a sudden, while I'm making my lunch or starting the car or brushing my hair, my eyes just flood with tears, and my heart just starts to break. I don't even know what brings it on most of the time."

But sadness is just one aspect of depression's emotional spectrum. The disorder can trigger a host of other feelings, including:

Emptiness: A number of people with depression feel neither sad nor desperate but instead feel empty and unconnected to the world. Nothing, not even once-favorite activities or beloved friends, gives them pleasure. Nick used to love to golf with friends every weekend, and Jake looked forward to playing poker with his old army buddies. Now neither man feels much of a connection to other people, nor do they attain much pleasure from their hobbies.

"I try hard for my wife, but I'm just going through the motions," Nick admits. "I smile and laugh, just so my wife won't worry. Inside, though, I feel nothing. Not happy, not sad. Just there. I heard there was a word for that too: anhedonia, the inability to experience pleasure. That's me."

***Hopelessness*:** One reason so few people suffering from depression reach out for help is that they truly believe that nothing in the world could change their mood or their situation. The present is unbearable, and in their minds, the future can only get worse. Many psychologists believe that having such a sense of unconquerable hopelessness puts a depressed person at the greatest risk for suicide. Jake knew that the grief he felt for his wife had turned into something darker, but he couldn't reach out for help. "Later my daughter told me that all I said to her was 'It doesn't matter,'" Jake recounts. "And that's the way it felt to me. I just didn't care what happened anymore. Live, die, it was all the same."

***Remorse*:** If the future looks bleak to someone who is depressed, the past is a place filled with disappointment, darkness, and regret. "I get stuck in the past so much," Janet says, "and all I see is where I went wrong. Leaving my career to care for the kids, wrecking my marriage, it's all my fault when I'm like this. If I'd been stronger, if I'd fought harder, somehow everything would be okay. There's a part of me that knows it isn't true, that *I'm* not all bad, but I can't seem to get past this. It's how I feel."

***Guilt*:** Sometimes depression brings on a debilitating cycle of guilt, followed by diminished activity, followed by anxiety and then more guilt. Lacking energy and motivation, many depressed people fail to perform regular chores, fall behind at work, or neglect the people closest to them. This creates tension and stress, more reasons to feel like an unworthy failure. "I know that I'm not taking part in my marriage the way I should," Penny admits, "and that I'm hiding things—emotions—from my husband. That makes me feel even worse. I get all tense and anxious as soon as I wake up. I don't want to let him down, and I know I do. But I can't seem to help myself."

Suicidal feelings: There are probably very few people who haven't contemplated, ever so briefly, simply giving up and dying. Among those who are depressed, however, these thoughts often become pervasive and pathological. In Chapter 4 we discuss in more depth what psychiatrists and sociologists think about suicide, but for now it's important to stress that suicidal feelings among depressed older men and women should never be ignored. All too often they lead to tragic ends.

Cognitive symptoms

Apart from emotional changes, depression often interferes with the ability to think clearly. Because we tend to equate problems with memory or concentration with senility instead of depression, these cognitive changes can be particularly worrisome. They include difficulty with concentration, poor memory, trouble with decision making, and general slowness of thought—the very symptoms we often associate with Alzheimer's disease and other types of dementia that occur in an older population.

"I was sure that my problems with memory and confusion were symptoms of my Alzheimer's disease," Dianne recalls. "I knew that I felt low and sad and couldn't shake a kind of exhaustion I'd never felt before, but I just assumed my descent into complete senility had begun. Luckily my doctor prescribed an antidepressant for me, and within just a few weeks I felt a hundred and ten percent better and clearer. I know that I'm going to have to face symptoms of Alzheimer's too, and probably pretty soon, but for now I feel as if I have a new lease on life."

According to government estimates, about four million Americans, most of them over the age of sixty-five, suffer from dementia, a general term, that has many causes. Although this number represents a small percentage of the older population, the pervading myth of senility in old age makes doctors, patients, and families quick to attribute cognitive difficulties to dementia rather than to a mood disorder. Dianne, for example, assumed her difficulties with memory and concentration were related to her recent diagnosis of early-stage Alzheimer's disease. Jake's daughter, Julia, felt certain her father had become senile because of the deeply confused state in which she found him.

What they both learned from their doctors, however, is that confusion and forgetfulness are often the first signs of depression in older people. In fact, some psychiatrists believe that a separate disorder called pseudodementia exists. Pseudodementia is a form of depression in which memory seems to fade and complicated thinking and concentration become difficult. The difference between pseudodementia and Alzheimer's or another dementia is that upon treatment with antidepressants, thinking returns to normal. In Chapter 3 we discuss the criteria by which physicians rule out dementia in cases in which cognitive changes present as the primary symptoms of depression.

Behavioral changes

When someone sinks into depression, behavior changes along with mood. Most of the time a depressed person withdraws from normal social activity and personal interaction. "Just the thought of having to talk to anyone oppresses me," Nick admits. "I avoid the phone, cancel my golf games, even try to get out of eating dinner with my wife sometimes. I just want to be alone, all alone." This pattern of behavior often results in a vicious cycle: The further withdrawn and isolated a person becomes, the harder and faster a depressive illness can take hold.

Many people tend to become not withdrawn but rather more agitated and irritable when depression takes hold. In some cases this irritability is related to the effort it takes to deny there's a problem at all. "I snap at my husband all the time, just for asking me what's wrong," Penny reveals. "I feel edgy and tense all the time because I don't *know* what's wrong, I don't *know* what's happening. While I want to find out very badly, I'm also very scared and so deny, over and over again, that anything's wrong."

A very common problem that often coexists with depression is the use of drugs and alcohol. In Chapter 3 we look in more depth at the connection between the two, but it's important to note here that an increase in the use of alcohol or drugs (prescription or over the counter) could well indicate or exacerbate depression.

Without question, each of us probably feels one or maybe even more of these somatic, emotional, cognitive, and behavioral symptoms in our own life. When you experience enough of those symptoms, over an extended period of time, however, what you have becomes not a mood but a disorder, one that undermines your health and disrupts your life.

Depression: Its Many Forms

As you can see, depression is a heterogeneous disease, which means that its symptoms and course vary from patient to patient. Its heterogeneity makes it very difficult to diagnose, especially in the context of other illnesses, as discussed further in Chapter 3. Here we outline the four major categories of depression: major depression, chronic dysthymic disorder, seasonal affective disorder (SAD), and bipolar disorder (depressed phase). Let's take them one by one.

Major depression

"There's no point in treating a depressed person as though she were just feeling sad, saying 'There now, hang on, you'll get over it,' " writes author Barbara Kingsolver in her novel *The Bean Trees*. "Sadness is more or less like a head cold—with patience it passes. Depression is like a cancer."

According to the National Institute of Mental Health, major depression is the single most widespread mental disorder, affecting 10.3 percent of Americans in any given year. Therapists frequently think of major depression in three different forms: melancholic, psychotic (agitated), and atypical. Melancholic depression involves symptoms of deep sadness and feelings of slowness and lethargy. The depression with which Janet suffers is a classic case of melancholic depression. She wakes before dawn, and her symptoms are most severe in the morning, then lessen as the day wears on. She has no appetite—for food or for life—and withdraws from social contact as much as possible.

Penny's depression might be classified as atypical. She is more nervous and fraught than sad, she's gaining instead of losing weight, and she feels better in the morning than as the day wears on. Her concurrent anxiety makes her highly conscious of people's opinions of her—especially her husband's—and she deeply fears being rejected by her family and friends because of her self-perceived shortcomings.

The third form of major depression is psychotic depression, a form of the disease more common in the elderly than in younger people. In addition to typical depressive symptoms, psychotic depression causes individuals to lose touch with reality and often to experience delusions and hallucinations. Jake suffers from a classic case of psychotic depression. For several weeks before his daughter found him in an almost catatonic state, Jake came to believe that someone was poisoning his food and that he couldn't leave the house or the house would burn down. Maude too, with her feelings of persecution and guilt, may be suffering from a psychotic depression.

Dysthymia

Also known as chronic depression or neurotic depression, dysthymia is a depression in which a person is bothered by mild but persistent symptoms most or all of the time for at least a year. People with dysthymia describe feeling ''under a cloud even on a sunny day,'' ''seeing the world as gray and foggy,'' or ''always feeling one stroke below par.'' The National

Comorbidity Survey estimates that about 6.4 percent of Americans develop this disorder at some point in life, and probably just as many older as younger people succumb to the condition. In fact, although dysthymia usually develops before the age of twenty-five, most people are not diagnosed until they reach their early forties, fifties, or even later.

Although the symptoms of dysthymia are similar to those of depression, they tend to be both milder and longer-lasting. Many people with dysthymia claim that they've felt low and depressed for so long they don't remember feeling any other way. Even after treatment about 5 percent of those with dysthymia never fully recover and remain sad for two years or more after their initial diagnoses. In late life, bouts of dysthymia tend to occur more often and with shorter periods of relative health in between. Many older people in fact suffer from chronic dysthymia that is never diagnosed or treated. Dysthymia often coexists with other mental disorders. The National Institute for Mental Health estimates that about 75 percent of individuals with dysthymia also have periods of major depression (a syndrome called double depression), panic disorder, anxiety disorders, or substance abuse. Other studies have linked dysthymia with attention deficit disorder, conduct disorder, and personality disorders.

Seasonal affective disorder (SAD)

For millions of people, the arrival of autumn signals not the pleasure associated with the scent of burning leaves or the refreshing crispness of the air but instead a darkening of spirit, a closing down of the soul. An estimated ten million Americans suffer from seasonal affective disorder, or SAD, and for them, the fall (and less often the spring or summer) is a harbinger of depression.

Emily Dickinson, a poet who lived in Massachusetts (a state known for its spectacular fall foliage—and its harsh winters) during the nineteenth century wrote this poem, which cogently sums up SAD's distinctive symptoms:

> There is a certain Slant of light,
> Winter Afternoons—
> That oppresses, like the Heft
> Of Cathedral Tunes—
>
> Heavenly Hurt, it gives us—
> We can find no scar,
> But internal difference,
> Where the meanings, are.

People with SAD usually suffer from the same depressive symptoms as others: feelings of sadness, helplessness, hopelessness, guilt, and mild illness. They tend to eat more than usual during this time, gain weight, and crave rich carbohydrates. They spend many more hours than usual asleep yet feel chronically exhausted and lethargic. Researchers believe that the amount of sunlight to which we are exposed affects the production and use of body chemicals, including serotonin and norepinephrine, the two neurotransmitters most associated with depression. In addition to benefiting from antidepressant medication and therapy, many people with SAD find treatment with phototherapy (exposure to bright light) extremely helpful in alleviating symptoms.

Bipolar disorder

Nearly two million American adults—about one in a hundred people—suffer from a bipolar disorder, which is characterized by periods of depression followed by extreme highs, or mania. The various types of bipolar illness account for about 20 percent of all depressive disorders. Unlike unipolar depression, bipolar depression affects men and women about equally. The average age of onset is about the late twenties or early thirties, and it is relatively rare for someone in late life to develop bipolar disorder for the first time.

The symptoms of bipolar disorder vary greatly from person to person. Generally the depressive symptoms are similar to those we've already described: sadness, low energy, such somatic complaints as headache and stomachache, and poor self-esteem. During a manic phase the mood is different: People report feeling elated, stronger and smarter than ever, and very passionate about life and their part in it. The "highs" of mania can be quite dangerous, with people taking more physical, sexual, and emotional risks than usual. However, some people with bipolar disorder experience hypomania, a less intense mood of well-being and confidence that does not significantly interfere with daily life.

"It was exciting but exhausting to have my mother as a parent," Janet recalls. "You never knew what to expect. I'd come home from school one day and she'd have redecorated and rearranged the whole house.

Three weeks later the dishes would start piling up in the sink and my mom wouldn't come out of her room for days. And she had a relatively mild case of bipolar disorder, or so the doctors said.''

The cycles of mania and depression involved in bipolar can vary greatly from patient to patient and even from year to year within each patients. Initially the periods between episodes of depression, or mania, and normal mood tend to be relatively short. In time the interval between emotional extremes may grow longer. About 5 to 15 percent of those with bipolar disorder experience rapid cycling, which includes four or more manic or depressive episodes in a year, each lasting at least twenty-four hours and ending with a switch to the opposite psychological state. In ultrarapid cycling, episodes of depression, mania, or hypomania may last only twenty-four hours or less.

Like unipolar depression, bipolar disorder may follow a seasonal pattern, with individuals sinking into depression at regular times each year, then swinging into a manic phase at the start of the next season. In general, the course of bipolar disorder during the life cycle tends to follow a downward path, with the disease becoming more debilitating as the years go on. In late life the manic phases of the disorder tend to diminish perhaps because its victims no longer have the physical stamina to experience mania. Janet has noticed that her mother's downward spirals occur much more often from a state of relative normality than from the sky-high moods of energy and zeal. As is true of all aspects of this disease, however, each individual experiences different patterns and rhythms of symptoms and side effects.

Major depression, dysthymia, seasonal affective disorder, bipolar disorder: The range of causes, symptoms, and courses of mood disorders reflects the highly complex nature of brain chemistry as it affects general health, personality, and social functioning. As complicated as depression can be, however, it isn't always the only mental problem involved.

As you'll see in Chapter 3, sorting out the symptoms to establish a diagnosis of depression is not always an easy task—even for doctors trained to do just that. Not only do somatic complaints often mask depression but many physical illnesses cause symptoms that resemble depression. Doctors must rule out these conditions before treating a patient for a mood disorder. Another complication involves the fact that depression often coexists with other psychological or neurological disorders. Penny, for instance, suffers with a concurrent anxiety disorder, while Dianne faces the challenges of Alzheimer's disease. Many elders—upward of one million—suffer from Parkinson's disease, a brain disorder that is often associated with depression. Fortunately, primary care physicians as well as psychiatrists and psychologists are receiving additional training and advice with regard to detecting depression in their older patients. In Chapter 3 we explore some of those methods with you.

Important Questions and Answers About Chapter 2

Q. My mother is seventy-eight years old and lives in a nursing home because she suffers from Alzheimer's disease. She's been holding her own for quite a while and seems to be in generally good spirits most of the time, but in the late afternoon, around five o'clock or so, she becomes very confused and upset. She cries and cries. Could she be depressed?

A. It's impossible to know what's troubling your mother without examining her. It could be that she's depressed, but it may be that she's suffering from what is known as sundowner's syndrome. Most common in people with Alzheimer's disease or other form of dementia who live in institutional settings, the syndrome got its name from the increase in confusion, agitation, and sadness experienced at nightfall.

There are several reasons this pattern of symptoms might occur. If they came on suddenly, you should make sure your mother receives a complete physical exam; it could be that a urinary tract infection or a disturbance in her blood chemistry is responsible. Find out if she's taking any new medication that might trigger such a response.

Some psychiatrists think that sundowning may be a sleep disorder caused by a disruption in normal body rhythms (a subject we return to in Chapter 4). In fact there is some evidence that sundowning may be more common in the winter months with earlier and longer darkness and subdued lighting, which link it to seasonal affective disorder. Others identify the problem as stemming from the sedation given in order to quiet patients, especially on evening shifts in many health care facilities. Sedatives tend to lower the ability of patients to maintain orientation and arousal, making confusion more likely.

The best thing you can do for your mother is to keep her environment as predictable and regular as possible

since it appears that unfamiliar activities or surround-
ings are particularly disruptive to those with sundowner's syndrome. In addition, talk to her doctor
about the medications she's taking and when they're
administered. It's possible that her symptoms could be
alleviated by a simple change in the dose or timing of
her medication.

Q. My wife died six months ago, and I'm still grieving terribly for her. Should I be worried that I'm depressed? How long does it take after the death of a
loved one to feel normal again?

A. The process of bereavement is quite complex,
and there exists a wide spectrum of "normal grieving." In most cases it would be hard to distinguish
major depression from bereavement during the first
few months after the loss of a spouse. You should ask
yourself how your grief affects your life and health.
Are you now able to enjoy activities that once gave
you pleasure? Can you eat and sleep in fairly regular
patterns? Are you able to communicate with your
friends and family? Can you manage to feel some
optimism and hope for your future? If you can answer
yes to these questions, chances are you just need a
little longer to work through your grief. Talk to your
doctor if you remain concerned. In the next chapter
we delve more into the subject of diagnosing depression in the context of grief and other psychological
and medical issues.

Q. As I look back on my life, I see that I've had
these periodic . . . moods, as I call them, pretty
much all my life, but for at least the last ten years or
so I often have very low energy and just shut myself
off from people as much as I can, sometimes for

months at a time. I still work and everything, but it's so hard sometimes. Could I be depressed?

A. It sounds as if you might be suffering from dysthymia, a type of depression that tends to be long-lasting yet with relatively mild symptoms. Even though you've been able to continue with your regular routine, it sounds as if you've suffered considerably. Perhaps it's time for you to seek some professional help. The good news is that treatment for dysthymia is almost as successful as is treatment for major depression. That means you have about a 60 to 70 percent chance of finding relief from your debilitating symptoms.

CHAPTER THREE

Tracking Down Depression

"I felt as if I were going mad, and I think my doctor thought so too," Penny remembers. "Everything hurt: my stomach, my legs. And I'd get these headaches. My doctor gave me all kinds of tests but couldn't find anything wrong. Finally she just kind of patted me on the head and told me to get more rest. That made me so mad I went to see someone else, even in the midst of all this pain. I just wouldn't be dismissed or ignored. My pain was real. I needed help."

Penny is one of the lucky ones. Her depression didn't keep her from seeking the help she knew in her heart she needed. As Chapter 2 says, many people, especially those in late life, fail to ask for the attention they need. Have you seen a doctor about your symptoms or mentioned to your physician that you might be depressed? If you haven't, you're not alone. The vast majority of depressed people never seek the help they need to get well. Of those who visit doctors about their symptoms, most never mention the possibility that their problems could be psychological in origin even if, deep down, they suspect it themselves.

Why do so many people resist the idea that a mental

illness could be at the root of their problems? There are several common explanations, both cultural and personal. See if you might be holding back for any of the following reasons:

Disbelief: Many, if not most, older men and women are far too quick to assume that a physical illness is causing their depression. Others figure they feel this way "just because they're old." Few believe that a mental illness like depression could ever affect them. "I held out for so long I broke down completely," Jake admits. "I thought I was just grieving over my wife or just getting old. Me and mental illness? Didn't even seem possible. I let everything go. I gave up. If my daughter hadn't found me, I don't know what might have happened."

For Peter, the object of his disbelief was not that he could have a mental illness but that he couldn't fix it himself. "Pull yourself up by the bootstraps, that was the way I was brought up," Peter says. "Sure you can have problems—who doesn't?—but that doesn't mean you run to a shrink. Anyway, here I was, a sixty-nine-year-old guy in great shape, with a beautiful wife, a healthy son, money enough to be comfortable. So what if I was a little down? I'd snap myself out of it. But the snap just didn't happen. I just kept going down. I became confused, unable to make decisions, even about my health."

Shame: Despite the fact that Prozac and other antidepressants are among the most prescribed drugs in the United States—millions of men and women take them just because they are depressed—depression and other mental illnesses still exist behind a veil of fear and shame. Perhaps it goes back to the days when the mentally ill were thought to be possessed by the devil or were shut away in unpleasant and poorly run institutions without possibility of cure. Or the blame might be better placed on the continuing false impression that a weakness of character rather than a medical illness causes mental and emotional disturbances. Whatever the reasons, many people still feel too ashamed of themselves, their symptoms, and their behavior to seek treatment for depression.

Guilt: Guilt is one of the most isolating and paralyzing of all emotions, and depression and guilt often travel hand in hand. One reason for this unfortunate pairing is that people who become depressed shut down both emotionally and physically. Eventually the inability to function undermines work, family, and social relationships and responsibilities. This results in a vicious cycle of depression, guilt over failing to meet expectations, followed by more depression. Guilt comes too from feeling that somehow you should be able to lift yourself out of depression by simply "pulling yourself up by the bootstraps," as Peter aptly puts it. When you can't, you blame yourself, adding to the tension, guilt, and disappointment—and further paralyzing yourself from taking action.

"I guess the hardest part for me comes in accepting the relapses," Janet explains. "Talk about guilt. I'm always sure it's my fault, that I'm not strong enough, that I'm letting my mother and my children down. I know intellectually that I'm not to blame, but I just can't help it."

Fear of rejection: "I wasn't only ashamed, I was also *afraid* to let anyone know how I was feeling," admits Dianne. "For the longest time I thought my friends would desert me if they knew the darkness and panic that flooded my brain or would think I was just plain crazy and put me away. After all, I'd already lost a couple of so-called friends when they found out I had Alzheimer's. But when I finally got the courage to talk about it, I found out that many of my friends had experienced these same feelings." This fear of being rejected or abandoned keeps many older men and women from seeking treatment—and receiving comfort—for far too long.

Unfortunately there does remain a great deal of misinformation about mental illnesses like depression, and you may very well face some skepticism when you explain your situation to the people in your life. "The fact is, I don't want my business associates to know that I'm taking medication or seeing a psychiatrist," Peter confesses. "You'd think in this day and age it wouldn't be a big deal, and maybe it wouldn't be if I were twenty years younger. But I'm in the financial management game, and a mental illness coupled with the fact that I'm nearly seventy might put me at a big disadvantage. I don't want to take that risk. That's probably why it took me so long to ask for help, and even now I feel I have to play it very close to the vest."

Helplessness: The very nature of depression is responsible for the number-one reason people fail to seek treatment. You may feel so hopeless and helpless that you have neither the energy nor the will to pick up the phone and make an appointment. "At my worst," Nick admits, "I figured, What's the use? Nothing will get better; there's nothing anyone can do. I'm sick; I'm weak. My son, Scott, was the one who finally got me to call a doctor, and he had to stand over me and practically force me to dial the phone. I'm glad he did, but it was tough. It was really tough.''

Getting Help

Today you have more choices than ever when it comes to getting help for depression. In most cases older patients start with their primary care physicians, who then refer them to psychiatrists or psychologists for treatment. That process may be difficult, however, depending upon the type of health insurance you have or if you currently live in a nursing home or assisted-living situation. Your situation may be further complicated by the fact that Medicare, which most people over sixty-five depend upon for their health care benefits, pays psychiatrists and psychologists poorly. Over the years this practice has discouraged mental health professionals from working with older patients and thus gaining both the understanding and experience needed to help this community.

''I know we're lucky because both of us have great insurance coverage through my father's pension,'' Janet remarks. ''But I have a friend, Anita, who had to fight tooth and nail to get help for her father, who was in a nursing home. She told me there was just one psychiatrist who came in once a week to treat I don't know how many of the two hundred and fifty residents there. And his main job was to dispense drugs, not to diagnose depression or help Anita's father deal with his feelings. Finally she found a good therapist outside the nursing home who would accept a lower than usual fee so that Medicare would pay. Now Anita picks her father up from the nursing home every Thursday and takes him to Dr. Cohen. It was very frustrating.''

Unfortunately the problems Janet's friend Anita experienced with her father are not uncommon—within and outside the nursing home setting. Many managed care policies that attract older Americans with fixed incomes set arbitrary limits on the amount of mental health services they pay for. Most cover only 50 percent of the costs of a fixed number of visits per year. If you're able, you may want to use your own funds to seek care outside your health insurance plan—as long as it's not Medicare, which enforces strict regulations. Among the professionals you'll want to visit if you suspect depression are general practitioners, psychiatrists, psychologists, social workers, and therapists. Let's take a look at each type of professional.

Primary care physicians: Otherwise known as your regular doctor, your primary care physician is probably a specialist in either family practice or internal medicine. Both types of doctor are thoroughly trained in all aspects of medicine, including psychiatric disorders to some extent. They can prescribe antidepressants and other drugs and may also be able to offer you some counseling. If you've been seeing your personal physician for some time, you may feel more comfortable talking about your problems to him or her—at least at first.

You should be aware, though, that not all primary care physicians are on the lookout for psychological explanations for symptoms, especially in their older patients. In one study 51 percent of physicians failed to diagnose depression in their depressed patients. If the patients came into the office complaining of somatic symptoms, such as headaches or stomachaches, and denied any emotional problem, doctors recognized depression in only 20 percent of the depressed patients. Primary care physicians were more likely to diagnosis depression accurately when patients who were asked were willing to accept the idea that their symptoms might be psychological in origin. Fortunately, if you're reading this book, you're more likely to visit your doctor with the idea that you might be depressed and thus have a much better chance of receiving an accurate diagnosis.

Nevertheless, no matter how comfortable you are with your primary physician, you may decide to seek help from a professional specially trained in mental and emotional problems. If your depression is complicated by another mental disorder, such as anxiety, or if you have underlying and recurrent psychosocial issues, you may require more intensive interpersonal counseling than your physician is able to provide. In that case a psychiatrist, psychologist, or other mental health professional may be your best bet. More than likely your doctor will be glad to recommend further treatment he or she thinks is right for you. Before you start treatment, however, your primary physician should give you a complete physical exam—described later in this chapter—and, if a diagnosis of depression exists, inform the mental health professional of any concurrent medical problems.

Psychiatrists: Psychiatrists are medical doctors who specialize in the diagnosis and treatment of mental or psychiatric disorders. Each has completed medical school, a year-long internship, and a three-year residency program that provides training in diagnosis and treatment of psychiatric disorders. Psychiatrists can prescribe medications and make medical decisions. Because older patients frequently take several different medications and thus may require close monitoring of their antidepressant use, many choose psychiatrists, who can prescribe drugs, over psychologists.

Psychologists: Psychologists have completed graduate programs in human psychology that include clinical training and internship in counseling, psychotherapy, and psychological testing. Although most have doctorates (either a Ph.D. or Psy.D.), psychologists have not studied medicine, nor can they prescribe medication. Most states require that psychologists be licensed in order to practice independently.

Social workers: Certified social workers (C.S.W.'s) or licensed clinical social workers (L.C.S.W.'s) have completed two-year graduate programs with specialized training in helping people with mental problems, in addition to conventional social work. Most states certify or license social workers and require them to pass qualifying exams. Many nursing homes offer their patients the services of social workers, who can be extremely helpful not only in providing psychotherapy but also in dealing with financial and practical matters that can often overwhelm older patients and their families. Indeed social workers frequently have more background and training in helping elderly patients deal with psychosocial problems than do psychiatrists and psychologists.

Psychiatric nurses: These health care professionals have earned nursing degrees and have special training and experience in mental health care. Most psychiatric nurses work in hospital or nursing home environments and thus have the opportunity to treat many older men and women with depression.

Therapists: The term "therapist" is used to describe almost anyone who helps people cope with mental and emotional problems, from board-certified psychiatrists to licensed psychologists to unlicensed (and largely unregulated) marriage counselors, hypnotherapists, and stress management specialists. Many of these people are highly trained professionals, but others are not. That's why it's important to check references carefully before undergoing treatment with any health care provider. (For the purposes of this book, we'll use the words "doctor," "therapist," and "counselor" interchangeably to refer to the person who treats your depression.)

In Chapter 6 we discuss finding a good therapist and provide tips on establishing and maintaining a good working relationship with him or her. In the meantime you need to take the first important step toward recovery: obtaining an accurate assessment of your problem.

The Diagnostic Procedure

Unlike the process involved in diagnosing most physical illnesses, no blood, urine, or X-ray tests exist to confirm or rule out depression. As mentioned in Chapter 1, your doctor or therapist will make a diagnosis by interpreting your symptoms and comparing them with a standard set of criteria, such as those in the *DSM-IV*. Now in its fourth revision, the *DSM-IV* has been the bible of psychiatric diagnosis since it was first published in 1952. It organizes symptoms according to disorder, taking away some—but far from all—of the once almost arbitrary nature of psychiatric diagnosis. At the end of this chapter we list the *DSM-IV* criteria for major depression, dysthymia, and bipolar disorder for your information.

As helpful as the *DSM-IV* is to therapists in making a diagnosis, it continues to have some drawbacks. One of its main disadvantages involves a relative exclusion of possible physical causes of symptoms. Unfortunately, conventional mainstream medicine continues to divide the body from the mind, the physical from the mental and emotional. The problem is that there really isn't a clear division between mind and body. As you'll see as you read this chapter, several physical illnesses cause, exacerbate, or—conversely—mask your emotional and mental problems. Indeed studies show that mental symptoms may precede the physical signs of some diseases by weeks, months, or even years.

At the same time the pain, isolation, and inactivity associated with illness can trigger a depressive episode that both you and your primary care doctor may overlook as you concentrate on solving the physical problems. Fortunately more and more primary physicians and psychiatrists alike are becoming aware of this complexity and thus make sure to take both psychiatric and physical problems under consideration with their patients' conditions.

The first thing your doctor will do is take an inventory of the symptoms, both physical and psychological, that have brought you to him or her. If you're a new patient, the doctor will also take your medical and psychological history and that of your family. This will help identify any patterns of illnesses in your own life or in your genetic makeup. Clearly, it is extremely important for you to be as open and honest with your doctor as possible. The more information you provide, the more accurate the diagnosis is likely to be. Here are some of the questions he or she is likely to ask:

1. What other illnesses do you now have or have you had in the past (i.e., cancer, arthritis, heart disease, thyroid problems, neurologic diseases, etc.)?
2. Were you previously diagnosed with depression or other mental illness? Have you had episodes of depression or bipolar disorder in the past?
3. Do you drink alcohol on a regular basis? Do you use illicit drugs?
4. What prescriptions or over-the-counter medicines do you take?
5. Do you have allergies to any foods, medicines, or other substances?
6. Do any illnesses like diabetes or heart disease run in your family?
7. What is your family history of mental illness, including suicide, bipolar disorder, and neurologic conditions like Alzheimer's disease?
8. What kinds of recent changes or stresses have occurred in your life?

The answers you give will help your doctor sort out the cause of your symptoms. At the same time it is very important for you to have a complete physical examination—with laboratory blood and urine tests—if you have not had one in recent months. Your therapist will either recommend that you see a primary physician or conduct the physical exam him- or herself if he or she is a psychiatrist and equipped to do so. This examination will help rule out any possible underlying physical problems you might have that could cause or exacerbate your depressive symptoms. He or she may also ask to speak with your spouse or a close friend to gain a better understanding of how your symptoms are affecting you, when they first occurred, and how they manifest themselves.

COMPREHENSIVE GERIATRIC ASSESSMENT OF DEPRESSION

History

Physical exam

Mental status exam, including cognitive screening
   instrument

Interview of collateral informant (spouse, sibling,
   adult child, close friend)

Personality assessment

Survey of prescribed and over-the-counter medications

Nutrition survey

Functional assessment of activities of daily living

Functional assessment of sleep habits

Assessment of social support activities

Routine diagnostic procedures

     Electrocardiogram

     Complete blood count

> Urinalysis
> Thyroid function tests
> B$_{12}$ level
> Folate level
> Glucose, electrolytes, BUN, creatinine chemistries
> Liver function tests
>
> Elective procedures to clarify treatment resistance or prognosis (EEG, CT scans, sleep study, etc.)

What to Consider First

Heart disease, a chronic and debilitating illness like arthritis that slowly saps energy and mobility, an addiction to alcohol that slowly takes control over one's life: These conditions and many others can trigger depression in susceptible individuals. At the same time the very same conditions may cause symptoms that resemble depression, and once the underlying problem is addressed, the depressive symptoms usually disappear.

THE LOOK-ALIKES OF DEPRESSION

Prescription drug reactions
Central nervous system disorders: Alzheimer's disease, Parkinson's disease, stroke, multiple sclerosis, epilepsy, and others
Cancer
Heart disease
Endocrine system disorders: diabetes, thyroid and parathyroid disease

> *Infectious illnesses:* hepatitis, bacterial and viral infections
> *Immune disorders:* systemic lupus erythematosus, AIDS
> *Substance abuse*

Probably the first thing your doctor will consider is the number and type of prescription medications you take. A number of widely used medications, a list of which follows, have been implicated in episodes of depression. (We discuss alcohol and illicit drug use later in this chapter.) Virtually any medication that slows down body systems or significantly changes body chemistry can cause depressive symptoms. These include drugs used to treat hypertension and heart disease, psychiatric drugs, over-the-counter antihistamines, estrogen, and steroids.

MEDICATIONS ASSOCIATED WITH DEPRESSION
(Talk to your doctor about *whatever*
medications you take)

Anticonvulsants: used to treat seizure disorders like epilepsy
      carbamazepine (Tegretol)
      phenytoin (Dilantin)

Antihistamines: used to treat colds and allergies
      diphenhydramine hydrochloride (Benadryl)
      any of a number of over-the-counter drugs

Antihypertensives/cardiac drugs: used to treat high blood pressure, angina, and heart attack
- clonidine (Catapres)
- guanethidine monosulfate (Isemlin)
- hydralazine hydrochloride (Aspresoline hydrochloride)
- propanolol hydrochloride (Inderal)
- reserpine (Serpasil)

Anti-Parkinsonism agents
- levodopa and carbidopa (Sinemet)
- selegiline (Eldepryl)
- bromocriptine mesylate (Parlodel)

Benzodiazepines: used to treat anxiety disorders
- clonazepam (Klonopin)
- lorazepam (Ativan)
- alprazolam (Xanax)
- diazepam (Valium)

Corticosteroids: used to treat arthritis and other autoimmune diseases, asthma, and cancer, among other conditions
- prednisone (Pred Forte, Deltasone, Orasone)
- cortisone

Hormones
- estrogen
- progesterone
- discontinuation of estrogen replacement therapy

Generally more women than men develop depressive side effects to medication. Women tend to become tearful and sad while men more often react with irritation and crankiness. Estrogen replacement therapy (ERT) during menopause seems to alleviate depression for many women, while causing it in others. Paradoxically, going off ERT may also trigger mood changes.

Apart from exposing us to the prescription drugs we take to alleviate them, severe and chronic medical illnesses themselves often trigger depression. At the same time evidence exists that severe or long-term depression may create a biochemical atmosphere in the body that makes us more vulnerable to disease. A report published in the *Journal of the American Medical Association* in 1991, for instance, found that patients with major depressive disorders who were admitted to nursing homes had a startling 59 percent greater likelihood of dying in the first year than those who weren't depressed.

Understanding the stress connection

What's the basis of this intimate connection between depression and disease? Scientists believe it has to do with the as yet poorly understood mechanism of what we commonly call stress, or the way the body reacts to physical and emotional stimulation. In fact, by studying the physiology of stress, researchers have been able to pinpoint perhaps the strongest evidence of a definite link between "body" and "mind."

To understand this connection better, think of a time when you were truly frightened, upset, or challenged (taking a driving test or meeting your in-laws). When you faced that challenge, didn't your heart beat faster? Didn't your palms sweat? Didn't you feel as if you might faint because the blood had rushed from your head to your feet?

In addition to anticipation and anxiety, what you were feeling was fear and anticipation—of failure, of rejection, of the unknown, perhaps even of success—and your body sensed your emotions. In a completely instinctive and interdependent way, your brain, your hormones, and your nervous system worked to prepare you to face what you perceived as a threat to your emotional, if not physical, safety. Whenever the body's internal balance is threatened, it mobilizes immediately, preparing you either to battle impending danger or to flee from it.

The fight or flight response requires the intricate coordination of two systems of the body: the autonomic nervous system and the endocrine system. The autonomic nervous system controls body functions like the heartbeat, intestinal movements, salivation, and other activities of the internal organs. The organs of the endocrine system, acting in conjunction with the nervous system, release stress hormones into the bloodstream that in turn produce various reactions in the organs and tissues of the body.

The most important stress hormones are norepinephrine and epinephrine, which stimulate the nervous system to raise blood pressure, continue to increase the heart rate and metabolic rate, and make you breathe faster to provide more oxygen to your muscles. Another stress hormone is cortisol, which works to increase blood sugar and break down protein so that you have energy for action.

As you can see, the body works hard to keep you safe from acute danger. Without this response, our cave-dwelling ancestors never would have been able to outrun (to say nothing of outwit) predators, and we need it today to stay safe from myriad threats to our well-being. The problem occurs when stress is long-lasting or we are already ill. In those cases the biologic and biochemical changes that take place during the fight or flight response can cause mental and physical diseases to develop; too much cortisol, for instance, is a risk factor for both depression and heart disease. Stress hormones also undermine the immune system, and that may allow the development of cancer cells to go unchecked by the otherwise alert immune cells. The changes to the brain's chemical balance that come with stress might be one factor in the development of degenerative brain diseases like Alzheimer's and other dementias. Stress also depletes serotonin and other brain chemicals involved in mood regulation.

When it comes to pain, so often a side effect of chronic illnesses and their treatment, the stress connection may also be a factor in the development of a related depression. With a long-lasting and disabling condition like arthritis, for instance, you can become "stuck" in the pain, caught in a cycle of frustration, fear, and exhaustion. If your hands hurt when you grip a golf club (as Nick's did) one day, and still hurt the next day, you become afraid of straining them further—so afraid that you try not to move them at all. Every movement becomes a struggle, one that finally undermines your confidence and energy. Eventually you become stuck within this cycle, unable to free yourself from the psychological damage that the initial pain wrought.

"Frankly I don't know which was worse, the ache of the arthritis or the way it made me feel about myself," Nick explains. "It got so I didn't know if I was just too afraid to try or if my elbows and wrists were too sore or what. Now that I'm doing some physical therapy, I feel better already, all around, mentally and physically. I guess I see that I have some control over my health, instead of the disease having it all."

As we'll see in Chapter 4, how stress affects our health remains the subject of intense investigation. For now it's important to understand that the mind-body connection is very real and that it sometimes makes diagnosing depression difficult in older men and women, who are likely to suffer from physical illnesses that cause or are exacerbated by depression.

In Chapter 1 the terms "reactive" and "endogenous" were mentioned in relation to the causes of depression. You can apply these terms here as well. Some people may experience depression as a reaction to becoming ill or being hospitalized. Natural feelings of sadness and sorrow are likely to follow a heart attack or stroke, for instance, because these events often affect our ability to function and our hopes for health in the future. At the same time they may trigger an endogenous depression because they change the biochemical environment in the brain.

What kinds of physical complications should you and your physician consider most when evaluating your symptoms of depression? Here are the most common diseases to look at when making a diagnosis of depression.

Central nervous system diseases

There's no doubt that a connection exists between diseases considered neurological in origin, like Alzheimer's disease and Parkinson's disease, and emotional illnesses like depression. As we discuss in Chapter 4, this connection is most likely the chemical substances in the brain called neurotransmitters. When these chemicals become imbalanced for any reason, they often have widespread effects. Brain tumors, for example, can also cause depressive symptoms, as can the side effects of many medications. Among the elderly, the most common brain disorders that cause symptoms that resemble depression are Alzheimer's disease and other dementias, Parkinson's disease, and stroke.

Alzheimer's disease and other dementias: Although losing mental capacity is perhaps the greatest fear associated with aging, the vast majority of people grow old without suffering any serious decline in their ability to remember or learn new facts. That said, about 15 percent of older people eventually do develop dementia, an organic brain disorder that interferes with their mental functions and that tends to grow worse with time. The incidence increases with age; about 50 percent of people over age eighty-five suffer some symptoms of dementia.

Approximately 50 to 60 percent of these individuals—about four million men and women over sixty-five—suffer from the type of dementia called Alzheimer's disease, while another 20 percent have vascular dementia, in which a series of small strokes damage or destroy brain tissue. Parkinson's disease also can cause dementia in the elderly.

Alzheimer's disease, the most common dementia of aging, is a progressive brain disorder that primarily affects the cerebral cortex, the cap of deeply grooved tissue in which the brain's higher powers are located. As the disease progresses, memory, speech, and other aspects of cortical functioning begin to diminish. The progress may be slow or fast, but it is relentless and eventually devastating, and the search for the cause and cure continues to consume the attention of thousands of researchers in laboratories around the world. Scientists have discovered genes associated with a high risk for Alzheimer's disease. Some evidence points to a virus or some other external pathogen as the trigger for the degeneration, while still other research indicates that a combination of factors may be implicated.

At this point, however, no cure exists, and only a few treatments prove successful in alleviating symptoms. Low doses of antipsychotic medications, for instance, can sometimes help calm symptoms of anxiety and agitation as well as moderate the occurrence of hallucinations. In the early 1990s scientists developed a new drug specifically for Alzheimer's disease. Called tacrine (Cognex), the medication works by inhibiting the enzyme cholinesterase, which allows levels of an important brain chemical called acetylcholine to rise. Acetylcholine helps the brain retain and retrieve memory, and about 30 percent of Alzheimer's patients find that tacrine helps slow the progress of their memory loss. More recently the medication Aricept has become available. It works in a similar way to tacrine but is less likely to have side effects.

As discussed, an imbalance of brain chemicals like acetylcholine has widespread effects on mental and physical health. It should come as no surprise, then, to learn that depression affects as many as 70 percent of people with Alzheimer's disease—not simply because they become depressed about having the disease but possibly because the disease process itself may directly affect mood.

Since some of the early signs of dementia—insomnia, irritability, decreased energy—sometimes mimic those of depression and vice versa, doctors and patients alike often have a difficult time discerning symptoms of depression from symptoms of Alzheimer's. In some cases brain scans such as positron-emission tomography (PET) scans and magnetic resonance imaging (MRI) may help pinpoint pathologic changes in the brain if they have occurred. Fortunately there are also some factors that are characteristic of each disorder, especially as each one progresses.

Characteristic	Depression (Pseudodementia)	Dementia
Similarities		
Self-care	Lacking	Lacking
Restlessness	Present	Present
Irritability	Present	Present
Creativity	Lacking	Lacking
Somatic complaints	Present	Present
Orientation	Disturbed	Disturbed
Memory and concentration	Disturbed	Disturbed
Differences		
Onset	Quite abrupt	Insidious
Progression	Usually rapid	Usually slow

Awareness of problem	Usually aware	Often unaware
Memory loss	Complains of it	Tries to hide it
Mood	Depressed	Normal
Psychiatric history	Often present	Often lacking
Suicide risk	Considerable	Much lower

Unfortunately, as is true for depression, there exists no blood or laboratory test that will confirm if your symptoms are due to Alzheimer's disease, depression, or both. Instead your doctor will observe your symptoms carefully over a month or two or perhaps prescribe an antidepressant to see if that helps alleviate your mental and physical problems.

Parkinson's disease: About one million American men and women, most of them over the age of sixty-five, suffer from Parkinson's disease (PD), a neurodegenerative disease. In PD a part of the brain called the substantia nigra begins to degenerate and is thus unable to produce an important neurotransmitter called dopamine. Dopamine is a brain chemical primarily responsible for sending messages to the parts of the brain responsible for movement but also for some aspects of emotion.

SIGNS AND SYMPTOMS OF PARKINSON'S DISEASE

Primary Symptoms
- Tremor
- Rigidity (stiffness)
- Bradykinesia (decreased movement)
- Postural instability (unsteadiness/falling)

Secondary Signs
- Gait disturbances
- Dexterity and coordination difficulties
- Speech and swallowing difficulties
- Visual symptoms
- Pain and sensory discomfort
- Sexual difficulties
- Blood pressure changes
- Dermatological changes
- Gastrointestinal disturbances
- Depression
- Dementia

In addition to causing changes in the brain that may trigger symptoms of depression, Parkinson's disease requires treatment with medications that may cause psychiatric symptoms, including depression. Diagnosis and treatment of any underlying depression are essential. As is true for virtually every illness—physical or mental—depression will worsen the course and, significantly, the quality of life for the patient.

"I saw it happen, for sure, in my neighbor," Maude recalls. "Joe had Parkinson's disease, had it for about fifteen years, I think, and then, almost out of nowhere it seemed, he started to fail rapidly. He wouldn't eat, he wouldn't get up for his exercises. He slept all the time. His wife was at her wits' end. She thought it was over, that the medicine wasn't going to work anymore. His doctor, though, figured out that Joe might be depressed and added an antidepressant to his day. In about a month or two he was already better. He still had the tremor, and they had to play around with the amount of medicine he took every day, but he came around eventually. He lived another eight years or so, I think.''

Stroke: According to the National Stroke Association, stroke attacks nearly 500,000 American men and women each year, killing 150,000 and forever altering the lives of the 350,000 who survive. An estimated 3 million stroke survivors live in the United States today.

Stroke is a form of cardiovascular disease affecting the blood supply to the brain. When physicians speak of stroke, they generally mean there has been a disturbance of brain function, usually permanent, caused by either a blockage or a rupture in one or more vessels supplying blood to the brain. In order to function properly, nerve cells within the brain must have a continuous supply of blood, oxygen, and blood sugar (glucose). If this supply is impaired, parts of the brain may stop functioning properly. Depending upon the parts of the brain damaged by the stroke, movement, speech, and memory may be affected, sometimes profoundly.

In the context of a major stroke, depression is in some ways a perfectly natural reaction, for both physiological and psychological reasons. In the case of a severe stroke that limits movement and speech, the patient may feel sad and anxious over the loss of his or her former independence and sense of self and over the physical and emotional challenges that lie ahead. Simply being in a hospital or rehab center can be isolating and demoralizing too. Furthermore, a form of stroke occurs primarily among the elderly in which arteriosclerosis (the narrowing of tiny arteries) prevents enough blood from reaching certain portions of the brain. These atherosclerotic changes may trigger what are sometimes known as silent cerebral infarctions, tiny strokes that cause psychological and cognitive deficits (such as depression and memory loss) but usually do not cause gross motor or sensory deficits (such as paralysis or loss of speech). In order to evaluate cerebrovascular neurological damage and depression, a doctor may decide to perform sophisticated imaging techniques (like CT, PET, and MRI scans) in an attempt to locate damaged brain tissue.

"Because cardiovascular disease runs in my family and my father died of a stroke," Peter says, "my doctor first examined me pretty closely for signs that I'd had a small stroke. After looking at some X rays, he decided that I was probably depressed. Better than the alternative, I guess."

Cancer

The second leading cause of death among men and women over sixty-five (after heart disease), cancer also has an interesting relationship with the disease of depression. Doctors estimate that about 20 to 30 percent of patients hospitalized with cancer are moderately or severely depressed, yet only about 2 percent receive any antidepressant treatment. That bewildering statistic may explain why the incidence of suicide in cancer patients is anywhere from two to ten times as frequent as in the general population.

Although we tend to think of it as a single entity, the term "cancer" describes more than two hundred diseases involving abnormal and uncontrolled growth of cells, and almost all of them may trigger depressive symptoms, in some cases even before a doctor makes a diagnosis of cancer. For instance, depression is often the very first symptom of the fast-growing and nearly always fatal pancreatic cancer. Central nervous system tumors, such as those of the left temporal and frontal lobes of the brain and of the limbic system (deep inside the brain), are also very likely to produce early symptoms of depression and irritability. (Please be reassured, however, that *less than 2 percent* of all depressions that are later diagnosed as physical diseases turn out to be cancer.)

In addition to the organic changes that may trigger depressive symptoms, individuals with cancer struggle with changing issues and concerns during the course of the illness. Shock, denial, and fear probably come first, followed by the need to absorb vast amounts of information about a complex and frightening disease and then to make difficult decisions about treatment. The stress of coping with the diagnosis and the treatment process results in major depression in about 20 percent of cancer patients, often within the first six to ten weeks.

There's no clear answer to why so many cancer patients suffer from clinical depression; like all aspects of depression, the reasons probably vary from person to person. We do know for certain, however, that receiving treatment for depression along with cancer treatment improves both the quality and the duration of cancer patients' lives. In one landmark study that followed advanced breast cancer patients for ten years, supportive group therapy virtually *doubled* survival times among those who took part.

Heart Disease

Depression and heart disease also appear to be pretty close partners. According to some estimates, more than 50 percent of all people with heart disease will suffer from major depression at some point in their lives, compared with about 20 percent of the general population. When depression in heart patients is left untreated, the disease progresses faster and more seriously than in patients without depression. A 1994 study published in the British medical journal *Lancet* found that depressed heart attack patients were twice as likely to suffer chest pains as nondepressed patients with the same degree of heart disease.

Exactly how and why heart disease itself might cause depression, or why depression makes heart disease worse, are as yet poorly understood. Some research indicates that the biochemical changes related to depression cause an increase in heart rate, even during sleep, as well as an increase in blood pressure and the tendency of the blood to clot (all caused by the increase in the hormone cortisol). Depressive symptoms, especially those that occur more in the elderly, like anxiety and loss of appetite, also have an impact on the cardiovascular system. In addition, we know that medications to treat its symptoms very often have depressive side effects.

"That's the first thing they looked at with me," Maude remarks. "I've been on a host of heart medicines ever since I had a heart attack back about twenty years ago. It turned out not to be the case, but they did think twice about putting me on an antidepressant.

Then they found one that wouldn't interfere with my heart medicine, and so far it's working fine.''

Endocrine Disorders

The endocrine system—the body system that produces the powerful chemicals called hormones—works in close cooperation with the nervous system. The intimate interaction between the two systems means that any disturbance in normal hormone levels can lead to a wide range of neurological and mood changes, including symptoms of depression. Indeed any one of a number of endocrine disorders, including hypothyroidism, hyperthyroidism, Cushing's disease, Addison's disease, Wilson's disease, diabetes, and hyperparathyroidism, produce depressive symptoms.

The most common endocrine disorder of late life—diabetes mellitus—is also the one most likely to lead to depressive symptoms. This disease involves the failure of the pancreas to produce enough insulin—the hormone that helps the body break down food and convert it into energy—and of body cells to use insulin properly. If left untreated or poorly managed, diabetes can cause low energy, weakness, irritability, and difficulty with concentration—all signs of major depression as well.

Another common culprit in the endocrine system is the thyroid gland. Located in the neck below the Adam's apple, the thyroid gland secretes hormones instrumental in almost all metabolic processes, controlling the rate of metabolism and the body's consumption of calories. The hormones stimulate growth, are essential for the normal development of the central nervous system, and enhance the action of the adrenal gland's stress hormones (epinephrine and norepinephrine).

There are two major types of thyroid disease: hypothyroidism (underactive) and hyperthyroidism (overactive). If your thyroid is underactive, your body processes are slower than usual, leading to feelings of fatigue or sluggishness, weight gain, slowed thinking, and dark moods—again, all common symptoms of major depression. Hyperthyroidism, on the other hand, means an overactive thyroid: The gland secretes excess hormone and thus speeds up the body's metabolic rate. Although a far less common mimicker of depression, hyperthyroidism may also have symptoms of irritability, weight loss, and fatigue.

Infectious Diseases

Many infectious diseases, such as pneumonia, hepatitis, and tuberculosis, can cause a variety of mood disturbances, including symptoms of depression. Chronic fatigue syndrome, an apparently new disorder that emerged in the late 1980s, has symptoms that closely resemble those of depression, including low energy, somatic complaints such as headaches and stomachaches, and mood disturbances. Acquired immune deficiency syndrome (AIDS) also may have symptoms related to depression, especially should the disease allow opportunistic infections of the central nervous system to take hold.

As you can see, there is a chance that your symptoms of low self-esteem, lethargy, hopelessness, appetite and sleep changes, low energy, and somatic complaints could be signs of a physical illness requiring a very different kind of treatment approach from that of a classic depression. That's why it's important that you have a complete physical examination before you and your doctor assume that you are depressed. What's more, your symptoms could be complicated by other psychological conditions.

When Depression Is Not Alone

Do you feel panicky and anxious? Do painful memories of a past trauma sometimes overwhelm you? Do these feelings coexist with persistent depressive symptoms? According to the Depression Guideline Panel, a group of mental health experts assembled by the U.S. Department of Health and Human Services, more than 43 percent of people with major depressive disorder have histories of one or more "nonmood" psychiatric disorders. The most common comorbid conditions (conditions that occur at the same time as depression) include drug and alcohol addiction, anxiety and panic disorders, eating disorder, and posttraumatic stress disorder.

Alcohol and Drug Addiction

Almost any chemical substance we ingest—from illegal drugs like cocaine and marijuana, to liquor, to prescription drugs—may affect our brain's chemistry and thus our moods. Like depression, addiction appears to have a genetic connection, with children of addicted adults more likely to develop addictions than those without such family histories. Also like depression, addiction appears to involve a disruption of brain chemicals combined with psychological and psychosocial factors.

Among the elderly, substance abuse of both prescription drugs and alcohol has reached epidemic proportions. According to a hearing before the U.S. House of Representatives Select Committee on Aging in 1992, an estimated 72 percent of hospital admissions of older people involved alcohol-related problems, and addiction experts say that up to 15 percent of Americans over age sixty-five will develop an alcohol problem when they retire or when their spouse dies. Widowers over seventy-five have the highest rate of alcoholism in the country.

When it comes to medication abuse, the problem is just as worrisome. While men and women over sixty-five make up about 12 percent of the U.S. population, they consume more than 30 percent of all prescription drugs and 70 percent of over-the-counter remedies.

Unfortunately the risk of becoming dependent on some medications increases with age. The aging body no longer metabolizes medicine as efficiently as it once could, and body organs tend to absorb more of the medication. In addition, many elderly people need two or more prescription medications to handle one or more ailments or chronic illnesses. One drug may counteract or strengthen the effects of another, thus increasing the potential for harm. In some cases older people receive prescription medications from more than one doctor yet fail to obtain accurate instructions for taking them.

With substance abuse, as with most of the other medical and psychological conditions that mask or trigger depression, the line between cause and effect is thin and wavering. Some researchers believe that many substance abusers first start drinking or using drugs to "self-medicate," to relieve painful mood symptoms. William Styron believes that he drank for most of his life in order to mask his symptoms of extreme anxiety, and it was only when he stopped drinking and allowed himself to feel that depression set in.

COULD YOU OR SOMEONE YOU LOVE HAVE A DRINKING PROBLEM?

Not everyone who drinks regularly has an alcohol problem, but if you can relate to one or more of these statements, you may want to discuss the matter with a health professional.

1. I drink to calm my nerves, forget my worries, or relieve depression.
2. I'd rather take a drink than eat.
3. I tend to gulp my drinks.
4. I've lied to someone about my drinking habits.
5. I drink alone.
6. I've taken a fall or otherwise injured myself while drinking.
7. I've been drunk more than three times in the past year.
8. It seems as if I need to drink more and more to get the same desired effect.
9. I'm noticeably more irritable or anxious if I'm not drinking.

10. My drinking has interfered with my financial, social, or medical priorities.

If people who suffer from depression or anxiety also have a vulnerability to addiction, the use of substances to alter their mood can become a vicious cycle. The physical, social, and psychological problems caused by substance abuse only bring people further down, feeling even more useless, hopeless, and sad and then needing more alcohol, cocaine, or other substances to lift them up.

Unfortunately this cycle is often missed by physicians treating older men and women. Part of the reason is that so many of the signs of a substance abuse problem in younger people—marital difficulties, problems at work, legal problems related to driving while intoxicated—will not be present in elderly people who are widowed, are retired, or do not drive. Among the signs that may appear instead are injuries or falls, malnutrition, liver function abnormalities, and confusion and mood changes—again, conditions that mimic many other medical problems.

Addiction and alcoholism are complicated disorders, with complex causes, courses, and treatment options, and it goes far beyond the scope of this book to cover these problems in any depth. Suffice it to say, it is extremely important that you give your therapist a complete and honest rundown of your use (or abuse) of alcohol or drugs. Only then can he or she make an accurate diagnosis and devise an effective treatment plan that works to address all your problems.

Anxiety disorders

Perhaps the most common mental disturbance affecting older Americans today—even more common than depression—is anxiety. According to the National Comorbidity Survey, as many as 25 percent of adult Americans may experience an anxiety disorder over the course of a lifetime. The term "anxiety disorders" is used to describe several different types of symptoms, including panic attacks (sudden, inexplicable terror), inordinate fears of certain objects or activities (phobias), or chronic distress and general diffuse feelings of fear (generalized anxiety disorder).

As is true for depression, risk factors for anxiety include one's sex and age. At any age women are more than twice as likely as men to experience panic attacks and generalized anxiety disorder. Among the elderly, studies show that between 10 and 20 percent of the general population suffers from the disorder, with rates higher in those who live in nursing home and hospital settings.

Although more than a third of all individuals who consult mental health professionals do so because of an anxiety disorder, many do not receive appropriate diagnoses, especially if they are elderly. Too often doctors dismiss the physical and emotional symptoms of anxiety as being "normal" responses to the stress of growing older, being ill, caregiving, retiring, etc. However, anxiety disorders are primarily biological illnesses, with underlying genetic vulnerabilities and alterations of brain chemistry. While difficult issues and conflicts that arise in one's life can trigger an anxiety disorder or exacerbate one that exists, they don't cause it, any more than the death of a loved one or the breakup of a marriage causes depression.

COULD IT BE ANXIETY?

As is true for depression, an anxiety disorder has physical as well as psychological symptoms. In addition to feeling worried and anxious much of the time, do you:

- Feel restless and keyed up?
- Become easily fatigued?
- Have difficulty concentrating?
- Find yourself more irritable and cranky than usual?
- Experience muscle tension and aches?
- Have difficulty sleeping?

If your answers are yes and these symptoms impair your ability to function in your daily life, talk to your doctor about your concerns. Treatment is available to help you.

Depression and anxiety often go hand in hand. Panic disorders now appear to be present in about 10 to 20 percent of men and women with major depression, and more than 30 percent of depressed people also suffer symptoms of general anxiety disorder. Again, the line between the two is unclear. In some cases the disruption of brain chemistry involved in depression appears to trigger the panic and anxiety attacks. In others, the stress of dealing with panic and anxiety can so demoralize, isolate, and stigmatize its sufferers they may well become depressed as well.

It is extremely important for concurrent anxiety and depression to be treated. The combination can trigger deeper and longer depressions and considerably raise the risk of suicide. Treatment of a comorbid anxiety disorder and depression frequently involves using a combination of medications and psychotherapeutic approaches.

Posttraumatic stress disorder

"The memories of my grandfather touching me didn't even enter my consciousness until recently, and I'm nearly seventy," explains Penny. "I wonder now how much of my life has been affected by these deep-seated memories. I'd already been treated once for depression when my first marriage ended when I was twenty-eight, but I didn't remember anything about the abuse until I started getting involved in a new relationship last year. Now I'm working on a whole bunch of issues I never knew I had."

Penny's experience is shared by millions of Americans. The lifetime prevalence of posttraumatic stress disorder (PTSD)—the term applied to any persistent and distressing response to a disturbing, threatening past event—is estimated to be about 5 to 14 percent. Originally "PTSD" was used to describe the difficulties experienced by combat veterans, but recently mental health professionals have applied it to victims of rape, sexual abuse, and physical assault as well. Symptoms of PTSD include vivid nightmares, recurrent or intrusive thoughts about the event (flashbacks, in which sufferers reexperience the event), anger, irritability, feelings of emotional numbness and detachment from others, difficulty in concentrating, and depression. Treatment usually involves both antidepressant medication and psychotherapy.

Eating disorders

Although we tend to think of anorexia nervosa as a potentially deadly disease that strikes only teenage girls, it appears that older people—especially older men—may suffer from a type of self-starvation that is every bit as lethal. A controversial study by scientists at the University of British Columbia in January 1997 postulates that the median age of death from anorexia nervosa is much older than we might expect: sixty-nine for women and eighty for men. And while at younger ages, anorexia victims are 90 percent female and 10 percent male, for those over forty-five, the rate for men more than doubles.

In the older population anorexia nervosa—a disease that causes its sufferers to starve themselves—may be hidden by other medical issues. Diseases like cancer, for instance, sometimes result in wasting syndromes in which the person cannot eat or retain food and thus suffers from severe malnutrition. A physician treating an older person with cancer, then, may miss the signs of an active eating disorder.

Like depression, eating disorders, which include obesity, compulsive eating, and binge eating as well as anorexia, involve a disruption of brain chemistry as well as psychosocial stresses. Serotonin, one of the main neurotransmitters associated with depression, is also implicated in most cases of eating disorders. As we discuss in Chapter 4, consuming carbohydrates helps boost serotonin levels, which may help lift mood and return some balance to one's self-perception.

Treatment of eating disorders usually involves a combination of medication (antidepressants) and psychotherapy. Again, as is true for all comorbid conditions, it is important for you to discuss any eating-related problems with your doctor or therapist at the same time that you address your depression.

Zeroing in on Depression

In Chapter 2 we looked at the three main categories of depression: major depression, dysthymia, and bipolar disorder (depressed phase). Once your doctor has considered the role that other conditions and illnesses, both physical and emotional, may play in your condition, he or she will check against the following criteria to narrow down your mood disorder. We list these criteria here for your information only. If you have any suspicion that the symptoms you're experiencing now might be caused by depression, talk to your doctor. Clearly, making a diagnosis of depression requires more than simply checking against a list of typical symptoms, no matter how well considered.

Major depression

According to the *DSM-IV,* your doctor should base a diagnosis of major depression on these criteria:

- At least five of the following symptoms—one of which must be depressed mood or loss of interest or pleasure—persist nearly every day for at least two weeks and represent a change from the way the individual has felt or functioned in the past.

1. Depressed mood (feeling sad or empty or seeming sad or tearful)
2. Greatly diminished interest or pleasure in all or almost all activities
3. Significant weight gain or loss without dieting (e.g., more than 5 percent of body weight in a month) or increased or decreased appetite
4. Sleeping much less or much more than usual
5. Slowing down or speeding up of activity that is observable by others
6. Fatigue or loss of energy
7. Feelings of worthlessness or excessive or inappropriate guilt, not merely self-reproach about being sick
8. Diminished ability to think or concentrate, or indecisiveness
9. Recurrent thoughts of death (not just fear of dying), recurrent suicidal thoughts without a specific plan, or a suicide attempt or specific plan for committing suicide

- The individual experiences great distress or impairment in social, occupational, or other important areas of functioning.
- Symptoms are not due to the direct effects of a substance (e.g., drugs of abuse or medication) or a medical illness (e.g., hypothyroidism).
- Symptoms persist for longer than six months after the loss of a loved one.

Dysthymia

According to the *DSM-IV,* a doctor should base a diagnosis of dysthymia on these criteria:

- Depressed mood, reported by the individual or observed by others, for at least most of the day, on more days than not, for at least two years
- At least two of the following symptoms when depressed:

1. Poor appetite or overeating
2. Sleeping less or more than usual
3. Low energy or fatigue
4. Low self-esteem
5. Poor concentration or difficulty making decisions
6. Feelings of hopelessness

- During the two-year period no symptom-free period lasting for more than two months
- No major depressive episode during the first two years of the disturbance
- No manic or hypomanic episodes (see pages 55–56)
- No other mental disorder (e.g., schizophrenia)
- No substance (drugs of abuse or medication) or general medical condition responsible for the symptoms
- Significant distress or impairment in daily living

Bipolar disorder

It is rare for individuals over the age of sixty to experience their first episodes, and thus receive their first diagnoses, of bipolar disorder in late life. Nevertheless, it can occur, and you and your doctor should at least consider the possibility that you suffer from bipolar disorder if your symptoms match these criteria, according to the *DSM-IV*:

- Depression as described under "Major depression" on pages 51–52 along with intermittent periods of mania as defined by the following criteria:
- A distinct period of an abnormally and persistently elevated expansive or irritable mood that lasts at least one week or requires hospitalization
- During this period occurrence to a significant degree of at least three of the following symptoms (four if the only change in mood is increased irritability)
- Inflated self-esteem or grandiosity
- Decreased need for sleep (e.g., feeling rested after three hours of sleep)
- More talkativeness than usual or feelings of pressure to keep talking
- Disconnected and racing thoughts
- Distractibility
- Increase in goal-directed activity (socially, sexually, at work or school) or physical and mental restlessness or agitation
- Excessive involvement in pleasurable activities likely to lead to painful consequences, such as buying sprees or sexual indiscretions
- Marked impairment in one's ability to work or engage in usual social activities or relationships or a need for hospitalization to prevent harm to oneself or others

- No direct effects of a medication, illicit drug, or medical condition

Important Questions and Answers About Chapter 3

Q. My father has Parkinson's disease and depression together. His PD symptoms are very mild, but is it more important to treat them than the depression?

A. Not necessarily. Both are serious conditions, and both require treatment. The good news is that there's no reason, at least in general, why your father's doctor cannot treat them both at the same time. In fact, if your father's symptoms of Parkinson's disease remain mild, taking an antidepressant alone might do wonders not only for his mood but also for his PD symptoms. Many people suffering with chronic illness report improvement in their symptoms after receiving medication for depression, partly because of the elevation in mood that takes place and possibly also because of the biochemical changes the medication triggers. In the long run, however, your father will probably take both an anti-Parkinson's medication, such as Sinemet or Parlodel, and an antidepressant if he remains troubled by depression.

Q. Which comes first, alcohol abuse or depression? In other words, does being depressed cause someone to drink or does drinking cause depression?

A. No one knows for sure, and it probably depends entirely on individual circumstances and biochemistry. Recent evidence suggests that there may be gender differences involved as well. A study presented at the June 1996 meeting of the Society for Epidemiological Study showed that in women, depressive symptoms may lead to alcohol problems over time, while in men problems with alcohol may subsequently lead to depression. According to the results of the study, which followed nearly a thousand adults for seven years, women initially classified as depressed were two and one half times more likely to have alcohol problems after three years than women who were not depressed. In men results suggested that alcohol problems appeared first and were more likely to lead to depression. In the end it probably doesn't matter which comes first. Both conditions require treatment in order to avoid serious health complications and diminish the likelihood of relapses.

Q. My seventy-year-old sister has no energy, she's lost interest in everything (and she used to be a fanatic moviegoer), and she has become something of a hypochondriac. I think she's depressed, but she denies it. Is it possible to be depressed and not know it?

A. Not only is it possible but it's common. Remember, there are any number of reasons why someone—especially someone your sister's age—might deny that her problem is emotional in nature; fear of rejection, shame, disbelief, and guilt are just a few. Because so many physical illnesses can cause symptoms similar to those of depression, your sister may also believe that it's easier or more ''normal'' to attribute her problems to a lingering cold or to just feeling rundown than to seek psychological help.

On the other hand, her physical symptoms may indicate the early stages of an illness. At any age it is never wise to ignore symptoms of pain, lethargy, or distress. Discuss your concerns with your sister as gently and compassionately as possible, and encourage her to see her doctor for a checkup and evaluation if she continues to feel poorly.

CHAPTER FOUR

Understanding the Biology of Depression

"I've heard a lot about what depression is and what it isn't, who gets it, when we tend to get it, and some of the reasons why," Penny remarks. "What no one's been able to tell me is *where* depression happens. Is it 'all in my head,' as the saying goes? If so, how is it that I also have problems with my stomach and with headaches? Where do my emotions live?"

Scientists all over the world continue to search for answers to Penny's insightful question. In recent years they've gathered much information that seems to point in the right direction. In fact medical researchers have dubbed the brain "medicine's last frontier" and the 1990s the "Decade of the Brain," estimating that they've learned a full 95 percent of what they know about brain anatomy and physiology during this decade alone.

What they've discovered about the aging brain is good news for all of us. The vast majority of men and women pass through late life retaining their mental capacities, especially if they keep their minds active by learning new things and challenging their imagination. At least biologically, healthy older men and women run no higher risk of developing depression or other psychological disorders simply because they're older.

As discussed in Chapter 3, scientists also now strongly suspect not only that a mind-body connection exists but that the connection is so intimate that we can no longer make a true distinction between the "mind" (thoughts, emotions, and memories) and the "brain" (tissues, chemicals, and nerve cells) and their effects on our physical and emotional health. In other words, feelings directly trigger physical reactions in the body, and physical changes trigger emotional responses. This understanding has led to more effective treatment for mental disorders since it recognizes both their biological and psychological aspects.

In this chapter you'll learn where in the body and brain scientists think depression takes hold and how physiologic and biochemical changes produce symptoms of sadness, emptiness, and physical discomfort. You'll see that three relatively new branches of medicine have emerged out of the Decade of the Brain, each offering some interesting theories about the way depression occurs in the brain and in the body. A branch of medicine known as biopsychiatry or neurobiology (and its applied sector, psychopharmacology), for instance, explores how brain chemistry affects mood and emotions and vice versa. Psychoneuroimmunology relates psychology (the study of behavior, emotions, and the mind), neurology (the study of the nervous system), and immunology (the study of the disease-fighting cells of the body). A branch of medicine known as chronobiology studies the importance of natural body rhythms to overall mental and physical health.

Later in the chapter we'll show you how these unofficial offshoots of modern medicine contribute to our current understanding of depression and other mental disorders. Before that, let's take a look at what science knows about where our emotions and moods live.

The Brain and Our Emotions

The human brain and nervous system form a vast communications network, one larger and more complex than the long-distance companies that span the globe. Every emotion we feel, action we take, and physiologic function we undergo is processed through the brain and the nerve fibers that extend down the spinal cord and throughout the body.

The brain itself is divided into several large regions, each responsible for certain activities. The brain stem, a primitive structure at the base of the skull, controls such basic physiologic functions as heart rate and respiration. The cerebral cortex is the largest and most highly developed portion of the brain. Divided into four lobes, the cortex is the center of the brain's higher powers, where the activities we define as "thinking"—thought, perception, memory, and communication—take place.

On top of the brain stem and buried under the cortex is another set of structures called the limbic system. Scientists believe this highly complex, and still largely unmapped, region is "home base" to our emotions. It receives and regulates emotional information and helps govern sexual desire, appetite, and stress. Three main centers of the limbic system are the thalamus-hypothalamus, the hippocampus, and the amygdala. The thalamus-hypothalamus forms a kind of brain within the brain, regulating a variety of human processes, including appetite, thirst, sleep, and certain aspects of mood and behavior. The hippocampus and amygdala help create memory as well as gauge emotions.

Thanks to the remarkable advances made in medical technology, scientists have been able to trace how the limbic system registers emotion and then produces emotional reactions in cooperation with other parts of the brain and body. Studies performed at the National Institute of Mental Health and published in the March 1995 issue of the *American Journal of Psychiatry* hint at the complexity of this process. These experiments show, for instance, that emotional opposites like happiness and sadness involve independent patterns of activity: When we feel happy, activity in the region of the cerebral cortex responsible for forethought and planning decreases dramatically, as does activity in the amygdala. When we're unhappy, on the other hand, the amygdala and another part of the cortex become more active.

This division of labor within the brain may be the reason we're able to experience a seemingly contradictory feeling like bittersweetness. At our grandchild's high school graduation we can feel both happy to see our own child, and her child, pass a remarkable milestone and sad at the loss of childhood and the relentless passage of time.

When it comes to depression, the studies show

something else quite interesting. It seems that the same area of the brain—the left prefrontal cortex—appears to be involved in both depression and ordinary sadness, but in different ways. It becomes more active during ordinary sadness but almost completely shuts down with depression. That might explain the emptiness and numbness many depressed people report. Furthermore, it appears that men and women may process sadness very differently. In women sadness causes much more activity in the brain than it does in men, a clue perhaps to how and why women tend to experience periods of more profound sadness than men and suffer twice the rate of depression at every age in the life cycle.

Sadness, joy, dread, regret, wistfulness, anticipation, awe: The extraordinary variety, subtlety, and depth of human emotion is perhaps our most treasured quality, and our ability to experience emotion our most precious gift. It is also a sign of health and vitality. When we are well, we have a full complement of emotions available to us. While each of us has his or her unique personality and range of moods, being healthy means being able to experience joy as well as sadness, anger as well as passivity, contentedness as well as frustration. For this to occur, brain cells must be able to communicate with one another, to send messages from one cell to another, from one center of brain activity to the next.

Mapping the synapse

How do the brain and body pass these messages among their various cells? Let's say you read about a grisly murder in the newspaper. How does the information pass through the parts of the brain that recognize letters and comprehend words and then go on to structures in the limbic system that trigger emotions like anger and fear? To answer these questions, scientists study not only the anatomy of the brain—its larger structures and organization—but also the biochemical processes that take place among the tiniest cells of the nervous system.

Each nerve cell, or neuron, contains three important parts: the central body, the dendrites, and the axon. Messages from other nerve cells enter the cell body through the dendrites, branchlike projections extending from the cell body. Once the central cell body processes the messages, it can then pass on the information to its neighboring neuron through a cablelike fiber called the axon. At speeds faster than you can imagine, information about every aspect of human physiology, emotion, and thought zips through the body from one neuron to another in precisely this manner.

But there's a hitch: The axon of one neuron does not attach directly to its neighboring nerve cell. Instead a tiny gap separates the terminal of one axon from the dendrites of the neuron with which it seeks to communicate. This gap is called a synapse. For a message to make it across a synapse, it requires the help of neurotransmitters, chemicals stored in packets at the end of each nerve cell. When a cell is ready to send a message, its axon releases a certain amount and type of neurotransmitter. This chemical then diffuses across the synapse to bind to special molecules, called receptors, that sit on the surfaces of the dendrites of the adjacent nerve cell.

When a neurotransmitter couples to a receptor, it is like a key fitting into a starter that triggers a biochemical process in that neuron. The receptor molecules link up with other molecules in the cell body, completing the transmission of the message. Once this occurs, whatever amount of neurotransmitter remains in the synapse is either destroyed or, in a process called reuptake, sucked back into the nerve cell that released it.

Scientists have named forty to fifty neurotransmitters and believe at least fifty more are yet to be identified. Each must be present in sufficient amounts for the brain and nervous system to function properly. When too much or too little exists, or if the cells are unable to use the chemicals properly, mental and physical disturbances may occur. Indeed biochemical balance appears to be an important key to mental health.

Neurobiology: The Chemistry of Emotion

"Behind every crooked thought there lies a crooked molecule," the late neuroscientist Ralph Gerard once wrote. The branch of medicine called neurobiology explores that very notion by attempting to identify, and then to resolve, the chemical imbalances that are often at the heart of mental disorders like depression.

As discussed, in most cases of mental illness chemicals called neurotransmitters—substances that allow nerve cells to communicate with each other—are not present in the right amounts or are not used efficiently. An imbalance of three neurotransmitters—serotonin, norepinephrine, and dopamine—appears to be involved in most cases of depression. These same chemical imbalances also occur in people who suffer from anxiety, eating disorders, obsessive-compulsive disorder, and several other psychological disturbances.

When it comes to depression, scientists have identified serotonin as the most common and likely culprit. With the most extensive network of any neurotransmitter, serotonin influences a wide range of brain activities, including mood, behavior, movement, pain, sexual activity, appetite, hormone secretion, and heart rate. People with depression have been found to have lower amounts than usual of serotonin in the brain, as have people with violent tendencies. As you'll see in Chapter 5, drugs that help more serotonin to remain available in the synapse—called selective serotonin reuptake inhibitors (SSRIs)—are often very successful in alleviating depression.

Another important neurotransmitter is dopamine, which follows two main pathways in the brain. One pathway connects to a portion of the brain called the corpus striatum, which controls movement. When this pathway malfunctions, as it does in such disorders as Parkinson's disease and Huntington's chorea, problems with muscle control arise. The other dopamine pathway extends into the limbic system. When dopamine does not exist in proper amounts or is unable to reach organs of the limbic system, emotional problems such as depression may occur. That's why so many people with Parkinson's disease suffer not only from movement disturbances but also from mood swings, emotional upsets, and, at times, cases of major depression.

Norepinephrine is the third neurotransmitter thought to be involved in depression. Lower than normal amounts of this neurotransmitter have been measured in people who are depressed as well as in people suffering with the eating disorder called anorexia nervosa. Scientists have found a few different medications that help restore proper norepinephrine levels in the brain.

Like serotonin, norepinephrine molecules contain only one of a certain kind of protein called an amine, so it is classified as a monoamine. One class of drugs developed to help alleviate depression concentrates on preventing a substance called monoamine oxidase from breaking down monoamines like norepinephrine and serotonin. When medication (called monoamine oxidase inhibitors or MAOIs) stops the action of this substance, more norepinephrine and serotonin are available to nerve cells, allowing cells to send and receive the right signals. Tricyclic antidepressants, discussed in Chapter 5, also work on restoring norepinephrine (as well as serotonin) activity.

As technology continues to improve, scientists will learn even more about these neurotransmitters and how they affect emotion, thought, and behavior. In the meantime they've already discovered that neurotransmitters do not work alone in transmitting messages but instead cooperate directly with another system of the body: the endocrine system, which produces chemicals called hormones.

The Role of Hormones

What lets your brain ''know'' that your stomach is empty and makes you feel hungry? What causes you to feel sleepy at night? Why does your heart beat faster when something frightens or excites you?

As you may remember from Chapter 3, the answer to all these questions is the same: Hormones, chemicals produced by the glands of the endocrine system, trigger the onset or termination of these and other actions and reactions. They work with neurotransmitters, chemicals that act as messengers, sending information and instructions to organs and cells throughout the body. In fact several chemicals are both neurotransmitters and hormones, depending upon where they work and what messages they are meant to transmit. Norepinephrine, for instance, acts as a neurotransmitter in the brain while it performs as a hormone on the heart and blood vessels during times of stress. Both hormones and neurotransmitters also work in tandem with the autonomic nervous system, cells throughout the body that take care of activities we think of as "involuntary," such as respiration, heart rate, and digestion.

When it comes to depression in late life, two areas of the endocrine system appear to be directly involved. The thyroid gland, for one instance, produces hormones that affect our emotions as well as regulate our metabolism. When the thyroid becomes hyperactive, it may produce symptoms that resemble mania: hyperactivity, overexcitement, loss of appetite, and insomnia, among others. When it becomes underactive, symptoms associated with major depression—excessive sleepiness, lethargy, and sadness—may occur.

The other important endocrine connection to late life depression is called the HPA axis because it involves the *h*ypothalamus, *p*ituitary, and *a*drenal glands. The HPA axis is involved in the regulation of cortisol, the stress hormone the body releases as part of the fight or flight response. Scientists studying depression discovered that a large percentage of seriously depressed people have much higher levels of cortisol in their bloodstreams than normal. Strangely enough, although depression often causes a *decrease* in feelings of agitation and activity (just the sort of biological state cortisol triggers), cortisol levels in depressed people are even higher than in people with disorders more commonly associated with extreme stress, like anxiety and psychosis.

As you'll see later in the chapter when we talk about chronobiology, cortisol is one of the many hormones the body produces on a relatively automatic, time-released basis. Some researchers believe that our internal rhythms of hormone production may become irregular and out of sync, causing a host of physiological and emotional symptoms. Another theory postulates that depression somehow causes the HPA axis to malfunction so that the body is unable to stop cortisol production after stress has passed. Suffering from prolonged stress, then, is a triggering factor for depression in many individuals.

Psychoneuroimmunology: Emotion and Disease

As the fight or flight response aptly illustrates, the body and mind are not at all separate but are one and the same. Your emotions are directly linked to your physical self. It should come as no surprise, then, that the way you think and feel about yourself and your life might have an impact on your physical health.

Think how often you've heard about one or more of these situations: A widow falls ill and dies within just a few months of her husband's death. A businessman working overtime under the stress of an impending deadline develops a head cold he just can't shake. A grandfather seems to will himself to live just long enough to see his granddaughter's college graduation. An otherwise secure woman succumbs to depression as she struggles to cope with chronic arthritis.

The new branch of medicine called psychoneuro-immunology presents a remarkable explanation for these seemingly coincidental events: Your nervous system is intertwined with your immune system, the cells of the body that fight disease. The activity of one system directly impacts on the other. One study conducted at the University of California at Los Angeles involved actors, individuals who by nature and training are able to elicit from themselves strong emotions on cue. As the actors experienced a certain emotion, researchers tested their hormones and blood to see what changes occurred. They found that certain white blood cells—cells important in fighting infection—increased in both number and activity level. This increase occurred no matter what kind of emotion, positive or negative, the actors evoked.

At first glance it might seem that having an emotional crisis could actually work to fight disease since it triggers the immune system to take action. But researchers postulate that the immune system becomes overworked if constantly stimulated, eventually losing its effectiveness and leaving the body open to disease. This would explain why illness tends to occur during, or immediately following, periods of stress. It would also show another link between depression and many physical illnesses: why it could be, as recent studies indicate, that severely depressed heart attack patients are about five times as likely to die within six months of leaving the hospital as patients who aren't depressed.

Exactly how thoughts and emotions act on immune system cells is still not fully understood. It appears that the brain is capable of triggering the immune system to perform in certain ways, the same way that the brain, when it senses fear, can trigger the heart to beat faster. Another connection between the brain and immune system involves chemicals called neuropeptides. Like neurotransmitters, these chemicals were once thought to exist only in the brain, but they have since been found throughout the body. According to current theory, these chemicals may be the physical representations of emotions. Neuropeptides control, for instance, the opening and closing of blood vessels in the face. When you suddenly feel embarrassed, these chemicals are responsible for the blush that rushes to your cheeks.

Precisely where does depression fit into the psycho-neuroimmunologic picture? That remains to be seen. For now, it is important to understand that calling depression a mental illness without recognizing its physical aspects is both arbitrary and ultimately self-defeating. It also behooves us to keep in mind that suffering from depression can leave us more vulnerable to a host of other illnesses, both psychiatric (like anxiety disorders or substance abuse) and medical (like heart disease and cancer).

Chronobiology: Timing Is Everything

Almost everyone living in the modern age has experienced what is familiarly known as jet lag. You arrive in Paris from Los Angeles after a grueling trip across three time zones. You feel disoriented, exhausted, even a little queasy and ill. You feel this way for a day or two until your body catches up with the local environment, until you feel tired when the natives feel tired and feel hungry just as the aroma of *pommes frites* wafts out of bistros at Parisian lunch- and dinnertime.

But what would happen if you never adjusted? If your body remained out of sync with your environment? What if there are events other than traveling through time zones, like a physical illness or an emotional crisis, that upset our body clocks? Many scientists, especially those involved in the study of body rhythms called chronobiology, believe that such unintentional disruptions do occur and may well be responsible for any number of mental and physical disorders, including depression.

Far more than we realize, our internal and external lives are regulated by rhythms: of light and dark, of sleep and wakefulness, of fluctuating body temperature, blood pressure, and hormone secretion. Researchers believe that our rhythms are driven by two different oscillators. One is very consistent and controls body temperature and many hormonal secretions; the other is more fluid and subject to change and controls sleep/wake and activity/rest patterns. Chronobiologists think when these two oscillators become desynchronized, illness—mental or physical—may occur.

What sets up these physiological cycles and keeps them on schedule? There are many different *Zeitgeber*s (as the term is known in German), or "timekeepers," that establish our body clocks. Some *Zeitgeber*s are internal, set up and maintained regardless of external factors (these are the more consistent ones). Others depend heavily on cues from the outside world: the knowledge we have of time established by clocks and watches (how often have we suddenly felt hungry only when we've noticed it's "lunchtime"?), the smell of coffee brewing in the morning, the sound of traffic picking up during rush hour in the afternoon.

Perhaps the strongest and best-known *Zeitgeber* is the sun. The light it brings each morning and takes away at dusk triggers the release or inactivation of certain hormones that affect our mood and behavior. For example, we don't go to sleep when it's dark only out of habit, or because darkness makes activity more difficult, or even just because we're tired. It's largely because the body produces a hormone called melatonin—also known as the chemical expression of darkness—when the eyes tell the brain that it is dark. Produced by a tiny endocrine gland in the brain called the pineal, melatonin then signals the rest of the body that it is time to rest. When the sun comes up, the body stops producing melatonin, and that produces the release of more action-oriented hormones, such as cortisol. Temperature and blood pressure begin to rise, revving the body up for daytime activity. That's why jet lag feels so odd. During it our bodies continue to produce "waking" hormones even when it's dark and to circulate "sleeping" hormones when it's light, until our external and internal *Zeitgeber*s have a chance to coordinate with each other.

Chronobiologists have discovered a number of fascinating things about how these rhythms affect our health. The length of time you sleep is related more closely to your body temperature and the time you went to bed than to how long you've been awake. Experiments show that even after having been awake more than twenty hours, people free of time cues slept twice as long if they went to bed when their temperature was at its highest (in early evening) than when it was at its lowest (in the early morning). Senses of hearing, taste, and smell tend to be most acute—strangely enough—in the middle of the night (around 3:00 A.M.), then fall off during the morning, then rise again to a new high between 5:00 and 7:00 P.M. (this may be one of the reasons why the evening meal in some cultures tends to be more sumptuous than breakfast or lunch).

Heart attacks are more likely to occur in the morning than in the evening. One reason is that more cortisol—the stress-related hormone that causes the heart rate and blood pressure to rise—is secreted in larger amounts in the morning hours than later in the day. Asthma attacks are also more likely to take place in the early morning, when lung function is at a daily low. Pain tolerance is highest in the afternoon; it might make sense for you to visit the dentist or participate in exercise or physical therapy at this time.

The chronobiology of age

One of the cardinal signs of a woman's passage into late life is menopause—the loss of estrogen, the primary female sex hormone. As her ovaries slowly stop producing estrogen, a woman's body undergoes a host of changes, starting with the loss of fertility. Because estrogen contributes to bone density, menopause brings with it an increased risk of osteoporosis, or thinning of the bones. The hormone also plays a role in skin maintenance (helping build collagen, the substance that gives the skin its "bounce") and in protecting women against heart disease. A very outward sign of aging (skin wrinkling) and a very internal sign (arteriosclerosis or hardening of the arteries) result. When the body stops its production of estrogen, the female body clock begins to slow down.

For men the start of the countdown is more subtle since testosterone production continues to some degree throughout the life cycle. Nevertheless, changes do occur and in a relatively standard pattern. In both men and women, aging and (eventually) death occur when cells within the body die or malfunction and are not replaced or repaired as rapidly as they should be. Eventually the system or organ affected by cell death or mutation will no longer be able to operate properly. Because human physiology is so interdependent, disruption in one part of the body often has widespread effects. The most commonly fatal diseases of aging— heart disease and cancer—as well as age-related chronic conditions such as arthritis and Alzheimer's disease all are related to what appears to be an inevitable loss of healthy cells and the chain of damage that results.

Scientists continue to explore what sets the process of cell death into motion in the first place. One theory is that every organism has an innate, species-specific life span. Most dogs, for example, have life spans of about twelve years, fruit flies approximately twelve months, and human beings about seventy-two to seventy-eight years. According to this theory, aging and death, like all other physiologic activities, are programmed into an organism's every cell. Exactly which and how many genes are directly involved in regulating human aging is still unknown, but some geneticists estimate the number to be about two hundred.

Another theory about the cause of aging centers on the endocrine system. Some gerontologists believe that somewhere in the brain there is an "aging clock" directly related to hormonal secretion. As discussed, the amount and type of hormones the body secretes change dramatically as we age. This alteration in hormone secretion eventually results in a body-wide imbalance that affects the health of our immune system, metabolism, and reproductive ability. We therefore become ever more susceptible to disease and disability as well as to the kinds of cosmetic changes associated with aging: wrinkling of the skin, loss of muscle tone, weight gain, and graying of the hair, to name just a few. One reason that older people are so vulnerable to depression could well involve a disruption in the rhythm of hormones and other brain chemicals related to mood and emotion.

The rhythms of depression
The science of chronobiology also explores the effect rhythms have on mental health. It seems logical to

assume there's a connection since so many of the classic somatic symptoms of depression—sleeping difficulties, changes in appetite and eating habits, poor concentration—are related to regular rhythms of life. Some are of these rhythms are circadian in nature— that is, they occur in cycles of roughly twenty-four hours. Blood pressure, heart rate, the sleep-wake cycle, appetite, some aspects of sleep itself, and body temperature are just a few examples of circadian rhythms.

Recent studies show that circadian rhythms in depressed people of all ages are significantly off kilter when compared with the daily rhythms of healthy individuals. Normal nighttime increases in melatonin secretion are absent in three out of four depressed people studied; in patients with bipolar disorder, the melatonin rhythm seems completely desynchronized, with more melatonin produced during depressive phases and less during manic periods. One reason for this disruption is that melatonin is derived from the neurotransmitter serotonin, which is also in an imbalanced state in most people with depression and bipolar disorder.

Sleep is what suffers most from the melatonin imbalance, with most depressed people sleeping much less or much more than usual. In addition, the pattern of sleep itself is different. Normally sleep consists of four stages plus REM (the near-waking state during which we dream). These stages occur in repeating ninety-minute cycles throughout the night, with REM occupying as few as ten minutes per cycle at the beginning of sleep, then increasing in length toward morning. With depression, REM sleep occurs far more quickly after the onset of sleep and diminishes toward morning. The lack of deep sleep itself and the strange, out-of-sorts feeling it leaves us with may well act as a trigger for depression as well. (In Chapter 8, we provide some tips for developing better sleep habits and patterns.)

One reason that older men and women are more prone to developing sleep problems is that the amount of melatonin the body produces declines with age. We start out producing very little melatonin as babies; studies show that rhythmic melatonin excretion does not begin until an infant is nine to twelve weeks old. By the time a baby is twenty-four weeks, total melatonin excretion is still only about 25 percent of adult levels. Slowly and steadily throughout childhood, melatonin excretion increases and becomes more regular—happy news for most parents since the baby finally settles into a standard sleep schedule.

Melatonin levels reach an all-time high during adolescence. Once full physical maturity has been reached, the pineal gland begins to shrink and melatonin levels slowly drop off. The older we get, the less melatonin the pineal gland produces and the rhythm of our days and nights changes profoundly. Some scientists believe that this change in rhythms is one reason that older men and women become more vulnerable to a host of physical and emotional ailments, including depression.

Some chronobiological rhythms are seasonal, although they tend to be more subtle in humans because they are exposed to indoor lighting and heating. Studies show, for instance, that more women conceive during the summer than in the winter in northern countries in which a strong seasonal contrast in light and dark patterns exists. This means that more babies are born in the inviting spring rather than in the dark, cold winter. Both men and women tend to eat about 220 more calories a day in the fall than in any other season, and even though they are eating more food, they feel hungrier at this time. Anthropologists suggest that we eat more during this time because we're unconsciously storing fat for the winter as we did long before refrigerators and freezers made food plentiful year-round.

Mental illness also has its seasons. Episodes of depression and bipolar disorder occur much more in fall and winter than they do in spring and summer. This tendency is so pervasive that the category of depression called seasonal affective disorder (SAD) has been created. As discussed earlier, about ten million Americans suffer with SAD every year, usually from October through April. Because the amount of light to which we are exposed lessens significantly during the winter, scientists believe that people with SAD may be particularly sensitive to the concurrent increase in melatonin secretion.

As the science of chronobiology continues to expand, we all may begin to understand better what natural rhythms mean to our mental and physical health. When these rhythms become desynchronized for any reason, we become sad, unfocused, out of sorts, ill. With medication, with therapy, or even through the physiological changes that come with the passage of time, most people can be helped. Others of us, however, are not. For such people suicide seems the only way to stop the pain.

Suicide: The Tragic End of Untreated Depression

"I just couldn't bear to be alive anymore," Janet says. "The pain, the emptiness, the look of pity and fear in my family's eyes. The thought of seeing myself in the mirror one more morning was unbearable to me. There was no hope. Nothing was ahead of me but more pain, more disappointment. So I hoarded some painkillers my son had left over from an injury and took them all one afternoon. If my sister hadn't come along when she did, I wouldn't be here today."

Janet, who attempted suicide seven years ago at the age of fifty-six, has come a long way since then. Although once again in the midst of a depressive episode, she has learned to recognize the danger signs and seek help before the despair and loneliness become too great. Janet is one of the lucky ones. At least thirty thousand people (some estimate the number is closer to seventy-five thousand) end their lives every year, and the overwhelming majority of them suffer from depression or another mental disorder.

Of that number, about sixty-three hundred are men and women over the age of sixty-five. That means nearly eighteen older Americans kill themselves every day. Indeed older adults have the highest suicide rate in the nation—more than 50 percent higher than young people or the nation as a whole—and this rate continues to climb, already increasing 10 percent since 1980 alone.

As discussed, the highest rates of suicide across the population are among older men. Twenty-five percent of all suicides occur in men over sixty-five. Male rates jump from about ten in one hundred thousand for young adolescents to twenty-five for young adults, then rising to about thirty-five for those age sixty-five to seventy-four and more steeply to about sixty in the oldest age group. In contrast, female rates of suicide are about five per hundred thousand during adolescence, about twenty in middle age, and then dropping to fewer than ten in the oldest groups.

Why suicide?

Contrary to popular belief, the average older man or woman who commits suicide is not poor, lonely, or extremely ill. Many, like Janet, have families; roughly one-third of elderly suicides are commited by married people and about one-half are committed by people living with other family members. In two-thirds of cases, they are in relatively good health and were recently examined by doctors. So then, we may ask, why suicide?

The answer appears to be, in almost all cases, depression. Without successful treatment, the feelings of hopeless and helplessness at the heart of depressive disorder overwhelm the affected individual, quelling any hopes he or she has of future happiness, future satisfaction—of any future at all. Like depression, suicide has a genetic (or at least familial) link. Relatives of suicides have nearly a ten times higher risk of suicide than those without such family histories. There also appear to be similar brain chemistry imbalances in those who are depressed and those who are suicidal—namely, a shortage of the neurotransmitters serotonin and norepinephrine. Research has shown that well over 95 percent of suicides' brains have deficiencies in serotonin, and—remarkably—the more violent (and thus more certain) means used to kill oneself, the lower the amount of serotonin in the brain.

DO YOU LOVE SOMEONE AT RISK FOR SUICIDE?

If you think someone in your life is considering suicide, follow these tips to help him or her stay safe:

DO . . .
. . . Take the signs and symptoms of suicide seriously.
. . . Ask the person directly if he or she is thinking about suicide.
. . . Get involved. Become available and show interest and support.
. . . Offer hope and alternatives.
. . . Take action! Remove easy methods of suicide (guns, pills, etc.) from the home and seek the immediate help of a trained mental health professional.

DO NOT . . .
. . . Be afraid to ask about suicide. Bringing up the topic *will not* cause someone to become suicidal.
. . . Dare the person to do it in an effort to snap him or her out of it.
. . . Discuss the moral implications of suicide or lecture on the value of life. Listen, but seek help from a mental health professional.

The gender gap for suicide is almost exactly the reverse of that for depression: Men are three times

more likely to take their lives than women. Elderly
men are ten times more likely to take their lives than
elderly women, and the incidence of suicide among
teenage boys is twice as high as among girls. However, while women are about three times as likely to
attempt suicide as are men, most of these attempts are
unsuccessful. One reason is that women usually
choose much less violent—and thus less successful—
means of ending their lives. Men are far more likely to
use guns or hang themselves, while women tend to
overdose on drugs or attempt to suffocate themselves
with carbon monoxide or gas. Because these latter
methods tend to take longer to succeed and are far
less certain in their effects, women are often saved by
intervening friends or relatives.

Why are women more prone than men to periods of
great despondency but able to survive the pain without ending their lives as frequently as men do? The
question may well be unanswerable. It could be that
women have ties to the earth and to other human beings that end up being too great to abandon; they give
birth, nurture both their children and their families,
are the caretakers. Most women seem to be able to
talk more openly about their feelings than men are
and thus are able to give and receive more support. It
also could be that something about the richness and
energy of their cyclical hormonal life keeps them alive
and willing to face another day, another season.

The question of euthanasia

"It hath been often said, that it is not death, but
dying which is terrible," the eighteenth-century British author Henry Fielding wrote, and many people

today believe that the right to take one's life in the face of unending pain or incurable illness is, or should be, inalienable. Yet evidence is mounting that the majority of those with terminal illnesses *do not* take their own lives, even if they believed they would do so before their diagnoses, unless they also suffer from depression.

"When I first found out I had Alzheimer's disease, I made a vow that I'd kill myself at the first sign that the disease had taken hold," Dianne admits. "But I didn't really start to think of it seriously until I became depressed. Then I obsessed: Could I hoard enough medication, would a friend help me if I needed her to, would I ever have the courage to shoot myself? I would think out these elaborate plots and strategies. . . . It was all I could think about. That's when I decided to get help. Now, that's not to say I haven't created a living will that clearly states my intentions about the rest of my life, and my death, but now I'm looking forward to using every bit of the brain I have left for as long as I can."

Many physicians treating older people fear that the rise in the availability of assisted suicide will lead to the unnecessary shortening of lives simply because a person whose depression goes unrecognized and untreated in the face of serious physical illness will too quickly succumb to the hopelessness and helplessness of his or her depression.

A topic as compelling as suicide—assisted or otherwise—deserves a larger forum than the one provided in this book. In the Resource Guide (page 252) you'll find a list of publications and organizations devoted to the topic. In the meantime it's important for you to understand, and thus be able to recognize, the risk factors and warning signs of suicide.

The risk factors and warning signs for suicide

A constellation of influences—mental disorders, personality traits, genetic vulnerability, medical illness, psychosocial stressors—combine to undermine an individual's strength and will to live. Depression and alcoholism are underlying factors in more than two-thirds of all suicides. Other risk factors for suicide include:

- Being a psychiatric patient
- Being an adolescent or being over the age of seventy
- Suffering from mental or psychiatric disorders, including depression and alcoholism
- Having a history of prior suicide attempts
- Experiencing a recent personal loss, especially in alcoholic individuals
- Having feelings of low self-esteem and hopelessness
- Having a family history of suicide in the last two generations

The three most common warning signs of suicide include:

- Extreme changes in behavior
- A previous suicide attempt
- Any suicidal threat or statement

Do any of the risk factors and warning signs apply to you or someone close to you? It may be a cliché, but it is one worth repeating: The best cure for suicide lies in prevention. If you believe you're at risk of taking your life, reach out for help. Talk to your physician, your therapist, your clergyman, your best friend. Do not try to face the darkness alone.

We've now come to the end of Part I. In Part II you'll discover that help for your symptoms of depression is available and—in the vast majority of cases— quite effective. It includes medication, psychotherapy, and aid from family and friends.

Important Questions and Answers About Chapter 4

Q. Psychoneuroimmunology sounds a lot like the "power of positive thinking." Can the way we feel or think about something really affect our physical health?

A. Scientists have known for decades that the immune system and the nervous system interact. When fighting an infection, for instance, immune cells are able to stimulate the brain to transmit impulses that produce fever. And receptors for many of the chemicals released during the fight or flight stress response have been observed on the surface of lymphocytes near the lymph nodes and in the spleen.

The power of feelings to affect the physical body was dramatically demonstrated in a study—cited in Chapter 3—performed during the 1980s and released in 1989. Dr. David Spiegel, a psychiatrist at Stanford University, divided a group of eighty-six women, with metastatic (spreading) breast cancer. One group was given standard medical care: surgery, chemotherapy, and radiation. The members of the other group received the same therapy but were also asked to meet once a week in a group therapy session in which emotions—often ignored by physicians concentrating on strictly physical aspects of cancer—were expressed, discussed, and confronted.

The immediate effects surprised few people: The women who had the support of fellow cancer patients and a qualified leader reported fewer symptoms of depression, anxiety, and pain than those in the other group. After all, they had more opportunities to express their emotions and find solutions to problems. What did surprise Dr. Spiegel and other physicians were the long-range effects of the support groups. Several years later Spiegel made a startling discovery: Those who had taken part in group psychotherapy—and suffered less from depression and anxiety—had lived twice as long after they entered the study as the group that had received only standard medical care.

How you feel, then, does have an impact on your physical health, and vice versa. It is important to understand that connection as you learn more about your own case of depression and how it may be affecting your health.

Q. You mentioned melatonin, the hormone related to sleep and the setting of the body clock. Is melatonin related to serotonin? Does it have a role in depression?

A. Melatonin is derived from serotonin, itself a derivative of a substance called tryptophan. Tryptophan is an amino acid, one of twenty-two organic compounds that are the basic building blocks of human life. Amino acids act as regulators of vital body activities—such as those that trigger the production of hormones like serotonin—as well as constitute the primary ingredients of muscles, bones, and other tissues. Melatonin and serotonin are inextricably linked; when melatonin levels drop or rise for any reason, so do serotonin levels, and vice versa. In people who are depressed, both serotonin and melatonin levels tend to be much lower than usual. In addition, scientists think that when the melatonin level changes, it disrupts the internal body "clock," the one that organizes and regulates our physiologic, emotional, and intellectual behavior. This disruption may be another important trigger for depression, especially in older people who naturally produce very little melatonin.

PART II

Treating and Coping
with Late Life Depression

The good news about depression in late life is that the disease remains highly treatable, despite the complications of coexisting diseases and intractable psychosocial issues. Using medication, psychotherapy, electroconvulsive therapy, or a combination thereof, doctors can help relieve depression in 85 to 90 percent of all older people. There's more good news: When depression is treated, coexisting problems may improve as well. Many people find that when their spirits are up, they experience fewer symptoms of chronic illness and fewer side effects of medication. They often have more energy and are thus more likely to participate in self-care regimens such as exercising, eating right, and following other medical prescriptions.

That said, there is no question that treating depression in older people often requires a more holistic approach than it may when the disease strikes younger people. Some doctors refer to a "geriatric syndrome" because depression in the elderly often takes place within a context of other illnesses or special circumstances. In such cases physicians, patients, and families must work together not only to alleviate the depression but to address other concerns as well.

Bereavement: Following the death of a spouse or other

loved one, a depressed person may not respond to therapy for an underlying depression until he or she receives counseling or support that addresses issues surrounding the personal loss.

Medical illnesses: As Chapter 3 outlines, there remains a close connection between physical and psychological illnesses—so close a connection in fact that even doctors find it difficult to differentiate the two or to treat one successfully without treating the other at the same time. Anyone suffering from depression must also receive care for coexisting physical illnesses, or chances for recovery are significantly reduced.

In addition to major medical illnesses, doctors, patients, and family members alike should be alert to signs of minor but stressful problems that are usually easily solved. Dentures that don't fit properly may pinch or slide, making talking and eating difficult and tedious. Constipation, which can develop as a side effect of medication or as a lack of fiber or water in the diet, may be painful and debilitating. If these types of problems don't receive attention, depression may linger as feelings of helplessness and discomfort mount.

Comfort issues: Unless you've faced a disabling illness or injury in the past, it may be hard to imagine how important to your health and well-being are issues of comfort and control. If you've ever broken a leg or arm, think for a minute about how that one injury affected your life: You couldn't shower easily or make the bed in the morning. Cooking was almost impossible, even brushing your hair (at least in the case of a broken arm) quite a struggle.

For an older person who's lost mobility or strength because of a chronic illness or surgery or through the ravages of time, these important acts of daily living can become painful and difficult not just for a month or two but every day for years on end unless someone intervenes with help. Imagine trying to regain hope and optimism if you can't open a jar or turn the faucet on your bathtub and being too embarrassed or ashamed to ask for help.

If you notice that you or someone you love is no longer as well groomed as in the past or no longer prepares meals as often as before, the issue may not be depression alone but may also involve physical strength and energy. Talk to a doctor or therapist for advice and help.

Accessibility: As discussed in Chapter 1, isolation is the single greatest risk factor for depression at any age, but especially in late life. In order to get well, many older depressed people need a way to reconnect with others, and that often means arranging for transportation to and from their homes and a senior center, adult ed classes, or even the doctor. Older people may not want to admit that they are no longer as independent as they once were, and doctors and family members should remain vigilant to signs that isolation is not a factor of depression but of transportation as well.

The complex physical and psychosocial issues of late life clearly deserve a larger forum than the one we provide here. The Resource Guide on page 252 lists organizations, like the Association for the Advancement of Retired People (AARP) and Eldercare, that can help you and your doctor address these matters as they arise.

In Part II we specifically focus on treating depression and its side effects. As you read about these methods, indeed as you take part in your own recovery, keep in mind that treatment of depression in late life often involves a wide range of goals, including:

- Alleviating symptoms and protecting against recurrence
- Improving quality of life
- Improving general health

- Considering a spiritual or psychological perspective for one's life and death

Chapter 5 discusses the medications now available to treat depression and the special considerations that come with treating with these powerful chemicals an older person who has depression. Chapter 6 explores the types of psychotherapy found most successful in treating depression as well as stressing the importance of coming to terms with one's life history. Chapter 7 focuses on how the disease affects the family dynamic and the special concerns for spouses and family members who act as caregivers. Finally, in Chapter 8, we show you ways to create structure and balance in your life through your recovery process and beyond.

CHAPTER FIVE

The Medical Arsenal: Antidepressants and ECT

"I know it's ridiculous, and I shouldn't feel this way," admits Maude, "but I've made it to eighty-three without taking any drugs for my mind, and I'm not about to start now." Suffering from severe depression with symptoms of persecution and delusion, Maude entered a hospital for treatment. Her daily sessions with a psychiatrist have helped her put her condition into perspective, but she still suffers from symptoms that her doctors believe require medical intervention, either with antidepressant medication or electroconvulsive therapy (ECT) or both. Maude, however, continues to resist. She is not alone.

Even today, as we head toward the twenty-first century, there remains a great deal of skepticism over, and disdain for, psychotherapeutic drugs of any kind. For many of the same reasons that men and women resist seeking help for a mental illness, they also resist taking medication. Some feel special shame that their emotional problems require drug therapy. Others believe that even if medication makes you feel better, it doesn't really count because you're no longer really "you." Others worry, usually needlessly, about unwanted side effects. And when it comes to ECT, the stigma is even greater, the fear even more pervasive—and just as needless.

Fortunately we've now had more than four decades of experience with antidepressant drugs and we know that for the most part they are quite safe. Their side effects are usually mild and tend to subside after a few weeks or months. We also know that they work for the vast majority of men and women suffering from depression, alleviating their symptoms and considerably shortening the course of depression. ECT has come a long way as well and is now the treatment of choice for patients who have serious concurrent medical conditions or who suffer from severe psychotic depression.

What we don't know is exactly how and why these medical interventions work. As we say in Chapter 4, the intricate workings of the brain and endocrine system remain somewhat of a mystery. Brain chemistry—the production and function of neurotransmitters—is particularly complex, and only in the last few decades have scientists learned enough about it to design drugs that help restore any imbalances that occur. In this chapter we describe what is now known about antidepressants and ECT and how best you can work with your doctor to receive treatment for your disease.

Before we start, it's important to stress that not everyone needs to take medication to alleviate his or her psychological disturbances. Penny, for one, decided against taking either an antidepressant or antianxiety medication, opting instead to work through the underlying issues with a therapist. "I'm not ruling it out," she says, "I just want to see how much progress I can make without medication. The truth is, just learning about what was happening inside me, and that it wasn't my fault, lifted my spirits a great deal. And the therapy has helped so much. Right now my doctor agrees that I don't need medication. Maybe down the line I will, but for now I'm taking it one day at a time."

Antidepressant Medications

Three types of drugs—each of which works to fine-tune the balance of neurotransmitters in a slightly different way—have been found to be most effective in treating depression: selective serotonin reuptake inhibitors (SSRIs), tricyclic antidepressants (TCAs), and monoamine oxidase inhibitors (MAOIs). There are also some drugs like buproprion (Wellbutrin), venlafaxine hydrochloride (Effexor), nefazadone hydrochloride (Serzone), and trazodone (Desyrel) that are not directly related to the others but are known to help alleviate depression. When depression is complicated by such psychological disorders as posttraumatic stress or anxiety, additional drugs may be used alone or in combination with an antidepressant. Benzodiazepines are the most commonly used antianxiety drugs, along with buspirone (BuSpar).

Later in this chapter we look at the specific uses, benefits, and side effects of these drugs in depth. In the end, however, all medication used to treat depression and related disorders has the same goal: to provide the brain with the raw materials it needs to send and receive proper messages about mood and behavior.

Before you decide to take medication

Although antidepressants are usually safe, they are still strong drugs that alter the workings of your brain and body. It is important that you consider the matter thoroughly with both your therapist and the doctor who prescribes the medication (if your therapist is not a medical doctor). Here are some issues to discuss with your doctor as you're deciding about drug therapy.

- *Make sure you tell your doctor about any other medications you take.*

As you may remember, eighty-three-year-old Maude suffers from a heart condition and takes heart medication that might be affected by the addition of an antidepressant. She also takes a blood-thinning drug called Coumadin, which requires her doctor to prescribe certain antidepressants with more care. Because Nick takes corticosteroids to soothe his arthritis, he too must be carefully monitored if he takes an antidepressant. As safe as most of the medications appear to be, there is always a risk of side effects when a patient takes more than one drug at a time.

Indeed any medication—even an over-the-counter drug—has the potential to modify your body chemistry and thus exacerbate an underlying health problem. In addition, there are certain drugs that may be dangerous when taken in combination with another or when taken with alcohol or, in some cases, with certain kinds of food. Before prescribing medication, your doctor should study your medical history and check your current health status. It's up to you to tell him or her about every drug—prescription or over the counter—that you take. This information will allow the doctor to prescribe the safest and most effective medication for you.

- *Tell your doctor if you think you have a problem with alcohol or other substances.*

It is absolutely essential that you tell your doctor if you are addicted to alcohol or any medication, prescription, over the counter, or illicit. Statistics show that between 10 and 30 percent of alcoholics become depressed over time, and the number is even higher for those with drug dependencies. As discussed in Chapter 4, some researchers believe that many people develop addictions to alcohol or drugs as a way to "self-medicate": to deaden the pain of their depression by biochemically attempting to correct a chemical imbalance in the brain.

If you think you have a problem, you must get help for both your substance abuse problem and your depression. It is impossible to treat one successfully without dealing with the other. In one study 60 percent of people admitted to a particular alcohol treatment program suffered with coexisting depression, but only 10 percent were prescribed antidepressants. A year later those whose depression had been left untreated were both still drinking and still depressed.

Depending on the severity of your addiction, your general health, and other considerations, your doctor may decide that you should enter a substance abuse treatment center or detoxify on an outpatient basis before starting treatment for depression. Most antidepressants have the potential to cause serious, sometimes fatal, side effects if taken with alcohol or other drugs.

If your substance abuse problem is relatively mild, and you believe you can stop drinking on your own or in combination with a program like Alcoholics Anonymous, your doctor may decide to treat your depression with medication as well as psychotherapy relatively soon. As is true for so much about depression, a decision like this one is highly dependent on individual circumstances and can be made only after the doctor performs a careful psychological and physical examination.

- *Find out all you can about every medication you take.*

Since depression often coexists with other medical and psychiatric disorders, particularly as you get older, you may be taking more than one drug. For each drug your doctor prescribes, ask and receive answers to the following questions (we answer some of these questions in a general way later in the chapter):

—What is the name of the medication, and how does it work?
—How and when do I take it, and when do I stop taking it?
—What foods, drinks, other medications, or activities should I avoid while taking this medication?
—What are the potential side effects, and what should I do if they occur?
—What should I do if I forget to take my medicine?

—How will I know if the medicine is working?

—How long will I have to take the medicine?

—Is there any risk that I could become addicted?

—Can you provide me with any written information about the medication?

—How much does the medication cost?

Listen carefully to your doctor's answers, and take notes on important points. Read all written material that is provided by your doctor or comes with the prescription itself. Follow all directions with care. Always remember that you have a right to know everything about the drugs you take and their expected effects and possible side effects. Armed with this information, you'll be able to make an informed decision, based on a full understanding of the risks and benefits, about whether or not drug treatment is right for you. Finally, make certain that you let every doctor who treats you know every drug you take.

- *Remember at all times that you are in control of your therapy.*

Many people fear that by deciding to take antidepressants, they are somehow giving control of their minds over to the drugs or to the doctor. Nothing could be further from the truth. In fact you may well feel in more control of your health—and better able to make healthy decisions—as you receive treatment for depression.

Unless you are terribly ill and incapacitated, you remain in charge of your own recovery from depression—whether or not you decide to take medication.

If there ever comes a time when you think that medication is not right for you, just let your therapist know. Unless your health would be seriously impaired, it is highly likely that he or she would accede to your wishes and taper off your medication appropriately.

Choosing an antidepressant

Which drug or combination of drugs will work for you depends largely upon your particular brain chemistry and constellation of symptoms. Since no test exists to measure exactly how one's brain chemistry is imbalanced or why it became that way, prescribing an antidepressant is often a hit-and-miss affair. Your doctor will decide which drug is best for you on the basis of an evaluation of your symptoms, medical history, and current coexisting physical or psychological problems.

When it comes to prescribing drugs of any kind to older patients, doctors also take into consideration the following factors:

Lower doses: An older body does not metabolize medication as efficiently as does a younger body, and thus the same dose of medication will result in a higher blood level of the drug. In addition, most elderly people tend to be more sensitive to the effects of medication. Usually doctors will prescribe *lower* starting doses of medication than they might with a younger patient with the same symptoms. In fact the slogan "Start low, go slow" is particularly apt when it comes to prescribing medication of any kind to older men and women.

More careful monitoring: Because many older people take more than one type of medication, doctors and patients alike have to be more vigilant in monitoring effects and side effects and guarding against drug interactions. Another reason to proceed with care is that the elderly run a high risk of overdosing on antidepressant medication. In some cases such an overdose will be a deliberate suicide attempt; as we noted in Chapter 4, suicide rates among the depressed elderly are quite high. Other cases of overdosing occur because the patient becomes confused or disoriented as a result of another illness (such as Alzheimer's disease or another dementia) or of a medication side effect and takes more of the antidepressant than is prescribed.

Flexibility: Once you and your doctor decide on a medication, it's important that you be as patient and flexible as possible. In taking an antidepressant, you are attempting to reestablish a proper balance of neurotransmitters in your brain. Needless to say, that's a pretty tricky enterprise that often requires a bit of finesse from your doctor and a great deal of patience on your part. It may take a few tries before you find the drug or combination of drugs that works for you.

In addition to these general guidelines, there are some special considerations for older people. In most cases doctors will prescribe lower dosages of certain antidepressants (specifically the tricyclics) for older patients, especially those with known cardiac conditions. Electroconvulsive therapy (ECT) is often used on severely depressed elders who may be unable to tolerate antidepressants, although this is rare.

After evaluating your symptoms and individual health profile, your doctor will decide which among the many medication options to try first. Depending on a variety of factors, he or she may decide to test your blood and perform metabolic studies on a regular basis to determine the effect the drug has on you. Following is a brief guide to the most commonly used medications used to treat depression and related disorders.

A Guide to Drugs Used to Treat Depression
Antidepressants

As discussed, antidepressants work to restore a proper balance of neurotransmitters in the brain, thereby allowing messages about mood and behavior to be delivered and received. They do so by acting to increase the available amounts of the serotonin, norepinephrine, and, to a lesser degree, dopamine. There are three main classes of antidepressants: selective serotonin reuptake inhibitors, tricyclic antidepressants, and monoamine oxidase inhibitors. Keep in mind that the dosages suggested here are for older patients— sixty-five and older—and lower than the doses commonly suggested for younger patients. Let's take them one by one.

Selective serotonin reuptake inhibitors

SSRIs are the newest of the three main categories of antidepressants. As the name implies, they work to relieve depression by selectively inhibiting the reabsorption (reuptake) of the neurotransmitter serotonin. The older antidepressants, called tricyclics, block the reuptake of both serotonin and norepinephrine. Prozac is the best-known and most commonly prescribed SSRI.

Selective serotonin reuptake inhibitors are often prescribed for the elderly because of their lack of side effects like orthostatic hypotension, a sudden drop in blood pressure that causes dizziness and—potentially—a dangerous fall. They are also often the best choice for people with such medical problems as heart disease, dementia, and Alzheimer's disease and certain other mental disorders, such as bulimia and post-traumatic stress disorder. Most people take SSRIs in just one or two doses every day.

General side effects: SSRIs may cause side effects in some individuals. They can cause nervousness or, less commonly, drowsiness, sleep problems, headaches, weight loss or gain, as well as nausea, vomiting, and diarrhea. Perhaps one of the most troubling side effects, one that affects about 10 to 20 percent of men and women who use SSRIs, is sexual dysfunction, including decreased sexual desire and delayed orgasm. (See Chapter 7 for information about coping with side effects of SSRIs and other antidepressants.) Finally, SSRIs must never be used in combination with MAOIs. Such a combination can cause serious, sometimes fatal reactions.

Fluoxetine (Prozac): *Dosage:* 5 to 10 mg/day once a day to start. If there is no improvement in two to three weeks, the dose can be increased by 5 to 10 mg/day up to a maximum of 30 mg/day.

Special considerations: Fluoxetine tends to be the most stimulating of the SSRIs and therefore may not be advised for someone recovering from a heart attack. Because it may interfere with the liver's ability to metabolize certain other drugs, taking it may heighten the effects of other medication. Fluoxetine stays in the body for a long time; just one dose can take up to fourteen days to disappear.

Paroxetine (Paxil): *Dosage:* 10 mg/day once a day up to a maximum of 30/mg per day.

Special considerations: Paroxetine may cause headaches, nausea, vomiting, diarrhea, dry mouth, and drowsiness. It tends to be slightly less stimulating than fluoxetine and does not stay in the body nearly as long (only about one day).

Sertraline (Zoloft): *Dosage:* 25 to 50 mg/day up to 100 mg/per day.

Special considerations: Sertraline usually produces less nervousness than fluoxetine and may interfere less with the action of other drugs.

Tricyclic antidepressants

Prescribed since the 1950s, tricyclic antidepressants (TCAs) were among the first drugs developed to treat depression. By slowing the rate of reuptake, they raise the levels of the neurotransmitters serotonin and norepinephrine.

General side effects: Weight gain is a common side effect of tricyclics; some people put on several pounds while using the drug. They also may cause dizziness or confusion, especially at the beginning of treatment. Flushing, sweating, allergic skin reactions, constipation, blurred vision, and anxiety are less common side effects.

TCAs block, to a varying degree, the action of the neurotransmitter called acetylcholine, which causes such side effects as blurred vision, dry mouth, constipation, orthostatic hypotension (feeling dizzy when standing up as the result of a sudden, temporary drop in blood pressure), increased sweating, difficulty in urinating, changes in sexual desire or ability, fatigue, and weakness. In addition, tricyclics can interact with any medications that affect the central nervous system, including allergy drugs, muscle relaxants, and sleeping pills. This is why it's important to tell your doctor about any medication you take.

Please note that each tricyclic works a little differently and thus may cause slightly different side effects as well. Amitriptyline (Elavil), for instance, may make you feel drowsy, while protriptyline (Vivactil) often has the opposite effect, causing you to feel anxious and restless.

Caution: Tricyclic overdoses—intentional and unintentional—can and do occur. Symptoms of an overdose of tricyclics generally develop within an hour and may include rapid heartbeat, dilated pupils, flushed face, and agitation. Confusion, loss of consciousness, seizures, cardiorespiratory collapse, and death may occur if these symptoms are left untreated.

Amitriptyline hydrochloride (Elavil): *Dosages:* 50 mg/day up to 150 mg/day.

Special considerations: Amitriptyline tends to be the most sedating of all antidepressants and is thus especially useful at night as a sleep aid. It is *rarely* prescribed for elderly patients since it can exacerbate any memory problems and confusion that already exist.

Desipramine (Norpramin): *Dosages:* 25 to 75 mg/day up to 100 to 150 mg/day.

Special considerations: Desipramine, which tends to be less sedating and more stimulating than other tricyclics, may cause anxiety, restlessness, and muscle twitches in some people. On the other hand, it is less likely to cause weight gain.

Doxepin hydrochloride (Adapin, Sinequan): *Dosages:* 25 mg/day up to 100 to 150 mg/day.

Special considerations: Like amitriptyline (Elavil), doxepin should be taken at night since it often has a powerful sedating effect. Also, like amitriptyline it is rarely prescribed for older patients since it can exacerbate memory problems and confusion.

Imipramine (Tofranil, Janimine): *Dosages:* 25 mg/day up to 150 to 150 mg/day.

Special considerations: Imipramine is known to produce most of the typical side effects of tricyclic antidepressants, including anticholinergic effects that may make it less desirable for older patients.

Nortriptyline (Pamelor): *Dosage:* 25 mg/day up to 50 mg/day to 75 mg/day.

Special considerations: Nortriptyline is especially useful for older patients because it has very few anticholinergic and orthostatic effects.

Monoamine oxidase inhibitors (MAOIs)

MAOIs work by inhibiting an enzyme called monoamine oxidase from breaking down neurotransmitters like serotonin and norepinephrine. Because they necessitate severe dietary restrictions, MAOIs are not usually first-line treatments for depression. They also can have very toxic, even fatal interactions with other medications. However, if a patient has been unable to tolerate or has failed to respond to SSRIs and tricyclics, MAOI treatment might be indicated. MAOIs may be helpful for some people with atypical depression—that is, sleeping and eating more than usual and feeling anxious.

General side effects: MAOIs cause similar side effects to those of other antidepressants, especially problems with orthostatic hypotension. They also react with certain foods and alcoholic beverages (such as aged cheeses, foods containing monosodium glutamate [MSG], Chianti and other red wines) and other medications (including over-the-counter cold and allergy preparations, local anesthetics, amphetamines, antihistamines, insulin, narcotics, anti–Parkinson's disease medication), and some antidepressants (particularly the SSRIs). If you and your doctor decide an MAOI is best for you, make sure he or she provides you with a list of foods and medications to avoid—and follow it to the letter!

Phenelzine sulfate (Nardil): *Dosages:* 15 to 30 mg/day up to 45 to 75 mg/day.

Special considerations: Phenelzine has a cumulative effect: This means the doctor may cut the dosage after a period of time. This drug is extremely dangerous when combined with cocaine and cocaine-related drugs and can cause serious adverse effects when used with Novocain or general anesthesia.

Tranylcypromine (Parnate): *Dosages:* 20 mg/day taken in two 10/mg doses.

Special considerations: Parnate may cause restlessness and agitation.

Atypical antidepressants

Some medications used to treat depression are chemically different from the three main classes of antidepressants. New drugs are being developed every day, but for now the four most common atypical anti-depressants are buproprion (Wellbutrin), which may target the neurotransmitter dopamine; trazodone (Desyrel), which targets serotonin receptors; nefaza-done (Serzone), which blocks a specific serotonin receptor subtype; and venlafaxine (Effexor), which works by blocking the reuptake of both serotonin and norepinephrine, but with fewer side effects than tri-cyclics.

Buproprion (Wellbutrin): *Dosages:* 50 mg twice a day up to 150 to 200 mg/day. No dose should exceed 150 mg, and there should be intervals of at least four hours between doses.

Special considerations: Wellbutrin is usually very well tolerated, causing fewer side effects than most other antidepressants. The risk for weight gain, drow-siness, and sexual dysfunction is much lower than for most other antidepressants. It does, however, cause seizures in a small minority of people—about four in every thousand who take it. Seizures are more likely to occur at high doses (over 450 mg/day). Like SSRIs and TCAs, buproprion cannot be used in combination with MAOIs.

Trazodone (Desyrel): *Dosage:* 50 to 100 mg/day when used in combination with an SSRI; 50 to 100 mg/day taken in two doses.

Special considerations: Trazodone is a highly sedat-ing antidepressant, which makes it useful for people with sleep problems who take it at night. It also ap-pears to alleviate sexual dysfunction in those who de-velop such problems with SSRIs. It may cause such side effects as dry mouth, constipation, and postural hypotension, as well as priapism (painful, persistent erections) in men. It should never be used in combination with MAOIs.

Nefazadone (Serzone): *Dosage:* 50 to 100 mg/day, given in two separate doses.

Special considerations: Like other SSRIs, nefazadone tends not to cause anxiety or drowsiness. It should not be taken by patients using MAOIs.

Venlafaxine (Effexor): *Dosage:* 25 to 150 mg/day, given in two or three divided doses.

Special considerations: In rare cases venlafaxine causes a rise in blood pressure, which may make this medication less desirable for older men and women with hypertension or other cardiac problems. It can also cause headaches and gastrointestinal symptoms like nausea, vomiting, and diarrhea.

Antianxiety Medications

Someone who suffers from a combination of depression and anxiety may be prescribed an antidepressant with sedating properties, in the hope that this antidepressant will have an antianxiety effect as well. Frequently, however, an antianxiety medication needs to be added to control the anxiety symptoms. However, antidepressants alone, especially the SSRIs, may help alleviate anxiety symptoms.

In the past doctors usually prescribed barbiturates for anxiety, but because of their addictive and sedating effects, other drugs were developed. Today most doctors usually prescribe either a drug in the class of medications known as benzodiazepines, used for both panic attacks and generalized anxiety disorder, or a separate drug called buspirone, used mainly for generalized anxiety. These work in slightly different ways to help calm and relax the anxious person and to remove the troubling symptoms of rapid heartbeat, difficulty with concentration, irritability, stomachaches, and breathing problems. Please note: If you are taking birth control pills, let your doctor know. The estrogen in the pill may reduce the effects of antianxiety drugs while increasing their side effects.

Benzodiazepines

Although highly effective in relieving anxiety symptoms, benzodiazepines can be addictive if taken for more than a few weeks. Benzodiazepines differ in duration of action in different individuals. They may be taken two or three times a day or sometimes only once a day. The dosage is usually started at a low level and gradually raised until symptoms are diminished or removed. The benzodiazepines tend to take effect quickly—within an hour or so. The hope is that these agents can be used to decrease anxiety temporarily while we wait for the antidepressants and psychotherapeutic interventions to work.

General side effects: Benzodiazepines have few side effects, and most that do occur tend to be mild and disappear on their own within a few weeks. Older adults with multiple medical problems need to work closely with their doctors. In some people these drugs cause drowsiness and mental slowing or confusion (that is why you shouldn't drive or operate heavy machinery until you know how you are affected by the medication). It is wise not to drink alcohol when taking benzodiazepines, for an interaction between the two can cause life-threatening complications. Be sure to consult with your doctor before discontinuing a benzodiazepine; a withdrawal reaction may occur if you abruptly stop. Withdrawal reactions are similar to anxiety symptoms themselves—shakiness, dizziness, sleeplessness—and thus may be mistaken for a return of anxiety. Your doctor will help you taper your dosage until you can safely stop taking the drug altogether.

Alprazolam (Xanax): *Dosages:* 0.25 to 1.5 mg/day up to 6 to 8 mg/day.

Special considerations: Alprazolam is known to relieve anxiety symptoms very quickly, sometimes within a day or two of taking the first dose, usually within a week. For depressive symptoms or for panic disorder, it may take two to three weeks for its full effects to take hold. Alprazolam can be highly addictive, and withdrawal is difficult. The drug should gradually be tapered off to minimize withdrawal symptoms.

Clonazepam (Klonopin): *Dosages:* 1.5 mg/day up to a usual maximum of 4 to 6 mg/day.

Special considerations: Klonopin too works very quickly to relieve anxiety symptoms and may help improve concentration and symptoms of lethargy that may accompany a coexisting depression. It is also used in bipolar disorder as an antimanic agent. Klonopin can be addictive.

Diazepam (Valium): *Dosages:* 2 to 5 mg/day up to a maximum of 40 mg/day.

Special considerations: Once one of the most widely prescribed psychotherapeutic drugs, Valium has been largely supplanted by other drugs, such as those listed above, that are less psychologically and physically addictive.

Buspirone (BuSpar)

Buspirone belongs to a family of medications called azaspirones and works to relieve anxiety by increasing serotonin activity in the brain. It is used primarily for the treatment of generalized anxiety disorder and is especially useful in treating anxiety associated with depressive symptoms. There is also some evidence that it may be useful in augmenting the effects of antidepressants.

Dosages: 10 to 15 mg/day divided into two or three doses, with increases up to a maximum dose of 60 mg/day.

Special considerations: Side effects, including dizziness, dry mouth, diarrhea, headache, nausea, and nervousness, are usually short-lived and mild. Buspirone tends to be slower-acting than the benzodiazepines, so it may take a month or to reap its full benefits.

Taking Medication

Believe it or not, the major obstacle to successful long-term antidepressant therapy is poor compliance—not concurrent illness or disability, not prolonged grief, not even drug interactions. The main problem is that 70 percent of patients—of all ages— fail to take 25 to 50 percent of their medication.

Many, if not most, people who take antidepressants find the process relatively easy and problem-free, especially after the first few weeks, when the drugs "kick in" to improve symptoms and most side effects have abated. Nevertheless, you'll no doubt have questions, now or as your therapy continues, about the drugs you're taking and how they are supposed to work. Please discuss your concerns with your doctor. In the meantime here are some tips about taking antidepressant drug therapy.

- *Give it time.*

Although you may experience some improvement, such as increased energy, within a week, it's more likely that you won't feel much of a change in mood for three to four weeks. If you need to increase your dose or try a different medication, it may take another few weeks for improvement to occur and even longer before you begin to feel the medication's full impact.

- *Monitor yourself for signs of improvement as well as for side effects.*

Taking medication of any kind requires a certain amount of responsibility on your part. It's up to you to tell your doctor how the medications seem to be working and what side effects (if any) they cause. The important thing is not to get discouraged. Many people need to try a few different dosages, different drugs, or even a combination of medications before hitting upon the right solution for them. Fortunately more than 65 percent of people who do not respond to one type of antidepressant will improve on another.

If you do not respond at all to the chosen medication or if you experience side effects that do not subside, your doctor may decide (1) to change the dosage, (2) to try a different drug in the same class of antidepressants, (3) to switch you to a drug from a different class, or (4) to try a combination of medications. If you feel only a little better on a particular medication at its maximum dose, your doctor might decide to augment your therapy with the addition of another type of drug, such as thyroid supplements or lithium. In addition, a short course of stimulants may help improve stubborn symptoms of fatigue and listlessness.

If your condition fails to improve and you are seriously depressed, your doctor may suggest electroconvulsive therapy (ECT). You'll find more information about ECT later in the chapter.

COMMON SIDE EFFECTS AND SOLUTIONS

Antidepressants often cause mild and usually temporary side effects. Often the symptoms dissipate within the first few weeks and then disappear altogether.

Side Effect	Solution
Constipation	Drink lots of water, boost fiber intake, get regular exercise
Dizziness	Rise slowly from a sitting or reclining position to avoid falls

Dry mouth	Drink lots of water, clean teeth or dentures often, chew sugarless gum
Headache	Take a mild analgesic
Nausea	Eat dry crackers or drink herbal tea; symptoms should pass within two hours of each dose

- *Report all side effects.*

As you can see by reading the information about antidepressants and other psychotropic drugs, side effects are common and often quite mild, and they usually disappear within a few weeks or months. However, in a few cases the side effects may persist and may undermine your health and sense of well-being. One of the most common side effects of antidepressants, particularly of some of the selective serotonin reuptake inhibitors (SSRIs) like Prozac, is a decrease in both libido (desire for sex) and the ability to reach orgasm. For reasons not fully understood, these drugs disrupt the normal pathways of sexual desire and function. Unfortunately, older men and women in particular all too often dismiss this side effect as either a natural consequence of depression or a natural result of aging, or both. The truth is, as we'll see in the coming chapters, sexual feelings are an important element of health and vitality at every age, and often a simple switch to another type of antidepressant will help you return to your normal level of sexual activity. In fact, because your depression will soon lift, you may find yourself enjoying intimacy even more than you have in the past.

- *Always follow your doctor's instructions with care, especially if you have to switch medications.*

As we've said, taking medication for depression tends to be a trial and error process. Sometimes, because the drug doesn't work effectively or causes unpleasant side effects, your doctor will prescribe a new medication. In some cases you can make the transitions immediately. In others you'll have to observe what doctors call a washout period to get one drug out of your system before introducing another. When doctors switch patients from an MAOI to a TCA or SSRI, they usually recommend a two-week or longer wait, depending on the drug chosen. Again, it's essential that you follow your doctor's instructions.

CAREGIVER TIPS

If you help take care of an older person with depression, here are some important tips about medication:

- Keep careful track of each drug, its schedule, and its potential side effects.
- Be consistent. Only one person—you, the patient, or another family member—should dispense the medication. Otherwise double dosing becomes a risk.
- If there's any risk of a suicide attempt, keep all medications locked safely away.
- Accompany your friend or loved one to the doctor when medication or treatment issues are discussed.

- *Talk to your doctor about how long you'll require medication.*

You and your doctor will decide together, on the basis of your current condition and how fast you improve, about how long you might need to remain on an antidepressant. As a general rule, once you've been symptom-free for about six to nine months, you both might decide to taper your medication dose while carefully watching for the recurrence of symptoms.

"That's been my mistake all along, I think," Janet says. "In the past when I've been through this, I'd take my medication and see my therapist religiously for about a year, but once I really got a handle on my life again, I'd stop—first the medication and eventually the therapy too. I'd hold it together for a while, but then I'd start to fall apart again. This time I'm going to stick with it for the two years my therapist recommends and see if I might stay better for longer.''

If you find that your symptoms recur, or if you have had recurrent depressive episodes in the past, you may require long-term drug therapy in order to stay well. Fortunately we know that long-term use of most antidepressants is safe; some people have taken antidepressants for as long as thirty years with no ill effects.

• *Avoid alcohol.*

Most doctors strongly discourage using alcohol while you are on medication. Not only does alcohol depress the central nervous system but it stimulates enzymes that break down the medication, lowering the amount in the blood and thus making it more difficult to maintain therapeutic levels. It also tends to enhance the sedating effects of antidepressants that cause drowsiness as an initial side effect. Furthermore, as noted in Chapter 2, alcohol is itself a trigger for depression.

• *Follow dosage prescriptions with care.*

Do not alter the dosage of any medication you take unless you have your doctor's explicit instructions to do so. Ask your doctor what to do under various circumstances: if you have a bad day, if you forget to take your medication, if you take more than the suggested dose, etc. That way you'll be less likely to suffer any adverse reactions should you take more or less medication than usual. Again, make sure every doctor who treats you knows about every drug that you take and when you take it.

• *Do not expect magic from your medication.*

It's important for you to understand the limits of medication. Although antidepressants can dramatically change the way you feel, you may well face other challenges, ones that drug therapy will not automatically allow you to meet. Depending on how severe and long-standing your depression has been, you may be suffering from low self-esteem, you may have learned nonproductive thought and behavior patterns to compensate for your blue mood and low energy, and you may have relationships in need of some repair. See Chapter 6 for more information about how psychotherapy can help you sort out your priorities and start you on the path to a fuller life.

Electroconvulsive Therapy: A Safe, Effective Alternative

Also known as shock therapy, ECT may be the treatment of choice for individuals with severe depression who are suicidal or delusional or whose disorder is life-threatening. The National Institute of Mental Health estimates that about 110,000 people each year receive ECT. When Julie first took Jake in to see his doctor, the subject of ECT came up almost immediately because of Jake's state of severe depression and his recent history of delusions and paranoia.

"Dad's doctor felt that my father was in grave danger," Julie explains. "He didn't want to wait for an antidepressant to kick in. He wanted a quicker solution. Because the idea of ECT frightened me a little, the doctor gave me some reading material, which helped me explain the process to my dad. In the end we all agreed it would be best. My dad went into the hospital and the next day started treatment. It took only about a week—three treatments—before I started to see a change. Pretty soon he was my dad again."

"I still have a ways to go," Jake admits. "And it sure scared me to death—made me feel like a real looney tune—to go through this, but it didn't hurt at all. Just made me a little fuzzy for a while. Now I can start to get on with the rest of it, the therapy and maybe some medication."

Scientists are unsure how and why ECT works the way it does to alleviate depressive symptoms in the thousands of people like Jake who undergo treatment every year. They believe that it alters receptors for the same group of neurotransmitters that tricyclic antidepressants affect, and they know it temporarily shuts down certain nerve pathways in the brain. Beyond that they just don't know.

Although the general public still harbors fearsome images of ECT—some of them promulgated by the excellent but outdated movie *One Flew over the Cuckoo's Nest*—electroconvulsive therapy is a simple and painless procedure. If you decide to undergo ECT, your psychiatrist will work closely with an anesthesiologist, who will place you under general anesthesia as well give you a muscle relaxant to minimize muscular response during the treatment. Usually patients receive about six to twelve treatments over a three- to four-week period in a controlled hospital setting. Your doctor will provide a regimen appropriate for you based on your individual needs.

With ECT you'll probably feel a little confused and perhaps agitated for short periods after each treatment. It is also likely that you'll experience what is called retrograde amnesia, a failure to recall events that occurred within a few months before the treatment. You may also find that your ability to learn and retain new information is hampered for several weeks. In all but one out of two hundred patients (as estimated by the American Psychiatric Association), memory returns to normal and memories of past events are recovered.

Who should have ECT?

In addition to people like Jake who suffer from psychotic and/or suicidal depression, individuals who might benefit from ECT are men and women who:

- Do not improve with either medication or psychotherapy or a combination of the two
- Cannot tolerate side effects of psychiatric medication because of their advanced age
- Have a medical condition that makes a rapid improvement in mood critical
- Have improved with ECT in the past
- Are malnourished because of their depression, to the point of being at serious health risk

Who should avoid ECT?

Although there are no conditions that absolutely rule out ECT, there are a number of people whose medical conditions would put them at risk for serious complications from the treatment. These include men and women who have:

- A mass in the brain (an aneurysm, a tumor, or stroke)
- An unstable spine, caused by fractures or displaced disks
- A seizure disorder
- A recent heart attack
- An acute infection
- Severe hypertension uncontrolled by medication

If you decide to go ahead with a course of ECT, your doctor will make sure that you have a complete medical exam and laboratory evaluation before treatment.

You've now received an overview of the medical options, including medication and ECT, available to treat your depression. In almost all cases of depression these options will work best only if you combine them with psychotherapy, which we discuss in depth in Chapter 6.

Important Questions and Answers About Chapter 5

Q. I suffer from diabetes, high blood pressure, and arthritis and now take trazodone for depression. I see two different doctors and have prescriptions filled at two different pharmacies, one in the health clinic and one around the corner from our house. I'm afraid of drug interactions. What can I do?

A. First, bring a complete list of the medications you take to each of your doctors, if you haven't already done so. Another thing you can do is use just one pharmacy to fill all your medications. By doing so, you'll cut down on the chances that you'll suffer adverse drug reactions or interactions for these reasons:

- A pharmacy creates a patient record or profile that lists every medication filled at that pharmacy but usually not at other locations. By sticking with one pharmacy, you and your spouse will have a complete record of medications, even those prescribed by different doctors.
- With this complete record, your pharmacist will be able to track potential drug interactions.
- By recording and reviewing your health conditions and past experiences with various medications, your pharmacist may be able to spot potential adverse drug reactions before they occur.
- When you need an over-the-counter remedy, your pharmacist can quickly check your record to help you find the best one to alleviate your problem without interfering with the medication you take for depression or other conditions.
- A complete record in one place may help answer questions for you or your doctor. For example, if you know a past medication caused adverse side effects but can't remember its name, your pharmacist will be able to track it down for you by looking through your health profile.

CHAPTER SIX

Psychotherapy Options

"I couldn't see myself in therapy, talking about my private business to a stranger. No way," Jake says with a shrug. "But between my daughter and my doctor, they convinced me to go to a bereavement group to talk about my wife. It was hard at first, but the other people—well, they're all pretty much like me, so I feel okay about it. I think it's helping me get better."

Nick felt a similar aversion to meeting with a therapist. "I just don't believe in therapy. It wouldn't work for me. I feel more comfortable with my regular doctor. He gives me medication and talks to me about what's going on. What's helped more than anything is finding a new medication and physical therapy program for my arthritis. Now that I feel better physically and I can play golf again, things have really turned around."

For Penny, recovering from her depression and anxiety wouldn't be possible without intensive psychotherapy. "My problems run so deep that I'm just finding out about some of them! For me, therapy is my lifeline. In fact I decided not to take medication, at least not for now. We're talking through everything now, and that's helping me a lot.''

As you can see from reading about the experiences of Jake, Nick, and Penny, psychotherapy is an important treatment option, but one that not everyone finds comfortable. Especially among the older people, there remains a strong resistance to the so-called talk therapies—and for many of the same reasons that keep them from admitting that their problems are psychological in the first place. Some harbor shame that they can't handle their problems themselves, while others fear the unknown aspects of psychotherapy (perhaps retaining the image of Freudian psychoanalysis in which old and painful memories are dredged up during years of therapy). Many people, like Nick and Jake, simply don't believe that talking to a stranger— even a professional—could possibly do anything to dissipate their deep despair.

Yet at the same time it appears that once older people overcome their initial reluctance, they benefit from psychotherapy every bit as much as their younger counterparts. Even in the midst of a chronic illness, or perhaps *especially* when a chronic illness complicates life, therapy can help identify the issues that contribute to the development of depression and other mood disorders.

If you're like most people suffering with depression, you too may have much to gain from involving yourself in one-on-one or group therapy. Indeed it is rare that psychotherapeutic drugs alone can solve the spectrum of symptoms and side effects—physical, emotional, and practical—that depression can cause. Many people harbor deep-seated guilt and confusion over mistakes they believe they made about treatment, for instance, or need help in identifying the sources of stress that helped trigger the depression in the first place. The disease creates a vicious cycle of low self-esteem that can be broken most effectively through therapy that helps identify sources of strength and confidence. Finding more positive ways to cope is a good reason to seek the help of a qualified therapist, especially in late life, when habits and ways of relating to others have become deeply entrenched. For many people, especially those coping with depression, psychotherapy helps put past mistakes, present complications, and future goals into perspective.

In this chapter we offer tips on what you should expect from therapy, finding a qualified mental health professional, and establishing a successful partnership with your therapist. As you'll see later in the chapter, many types of psychotherapy exist, each one addressing issues and concerns in a slightly different way. In the end, however, they all have the same ultimate objective: to help you reestablish connections with your full range of emotions—joy as well as sadness, pride as well as shame and guilt, strength as well as fear, anticipation as well as disappointment—and to look at the world and your position with more objectivity, optimism, and energy.

Defining the goals of therapy

Everyone—no matter what age—has a different set of reasons for seeking therapy and in the end derives different benefits from the process. Nevertheless, there are several issues that confront most, if not all, men and women as they get older, issues that may either trigger the development of or complicate the progress of a clinical depression. Among the most common and pressing personal and psychosocial concerns therapy can help you address are these:

Learning to cope with physical infirmity or impairment: One of the unfortunate consequences of getting older is the increased likelihood that illness or disability will strike. With a therapist you can discuss your fears of becoming ill or disabled, and the therapist can help you cope with any challenges that currently exist.

Developing a healthy attitude toward your own death: Because religious traditions have waned during the twentieth century, the concept of death may be especially difficult for men and women growing older today. Coming to terms with death in a way that allows you to face the future with a degree of realism and strength is another matter you may benefit from confronting with the help and guidance of a therapist.

Coping with the death of your spouse or friends: Even without the complication of a medical illness like depression, people grieving for lost loved ones can often benefit from the therapeutic process. Therapy can help you deal with any unresolved issues you may have had with the deceased as well as help you take steps forward to create a new life for yourself.

Developing the ability to form new ties: The people who adapt best to late life are those who can form new friendships and allow existing relationships to evolve even in the midst of enormous change. Retirement, for instance, often forces people to cut ties with colleagues and associates and form renewed relationships with spouses, children, and friends. Many older people move into smaller houses or apartments, gaining new neighbors at the same time. The loss of loved ones to death is an unfortunate but inevitable consequence of living long. Being able to form new friendships as death takes its toll can mean the difference between a lonely old age and a vital, meaningful late life. A therapist can help you lower any barriers to intimacy that may have built up over the years, thus leaving you more open to forming new relationships.

Coping with the reversal of roles with children and grandchildren: A natural but often difficult aspect of growing older is the change in roles played by parents and their children. Often, as illness or frailty eventually takes hold, an older person must relinquish some of his or her previous independence to his or her children.

"That's been the hardest for my father," Julie remarks about Jake. "He didn't mind being dependent on my mother, I guess because she was a peer, and boy, was he ever dependent. He honestly doesn't know how to do a laundry himself. But he hates having to ask me for help. I really want him to learn how to do that, because nothing would make me happier than to be there for him. I know he talks about that—and listens to other people's experiences—in his bereavement group. I hope it loosens him up a bit."

Coming to terms with the past: "For me what's become important, and overwhelming, as I near the end of my life, is putting all that's come before into some perspective," Maude remarks. "I sit up all night sometimes, trying to figure out what it means, if I did it right, if there's even a way to do it right. What am I leaving to the earth when I leave it?"

What Maude is trying to come to grips with—the

meaning of her life and death—is an issue that affects most men and women as they enter late life.

One goal of therapy for you may be to create an "autobiography," a life story that puts your past mistakes and successes, dreams and doubts into a philosophical perspective that has meaning and offers comfort. Talk to your therapist if the idea of doing so appeals to you; such activity is often quite therapeutic.

All these goals are important ones, especially to older men and women, not only because of their intrinsic worth to anyone getting older and facing the challenges of late life but also because sorting them out will help alleviate your depression. Indeed, no matter what your age or circumstances, you should look to therapy to help you meet the following goals:

To feel better: Needless to say, coming out of the darkness should be your prime goal if you're depressed when you enter therapy. You should aim to alleviate your symptoms of depression before you attempt to address any deeper or more complicated issues. Simply making the first appointment with a therapist may give you a feeling of positive control. In addition to talking through your problems and goals, you and your therapist may decide that medication can be another tool to help you feel better most quickly. Other strategies, which we talk about in further depth in Chapter 8, involve getting some exercise and reestablishing regular eating and sleeping habits. Your therapist can help you identify these strategies and offer advice about following through.

COMMON GOALS OF THERAPY

- Feeling better
- Identifying sources of stress or unhappiness
- Identifying and changing self-defeating thought patterns or behaviors
- Setting realistic goals
- Finding sources of support and learning to ask for help

To identify sources of stress or unhappiness: Once you've regained some of your energy and focus, you and your therapist can begin to look at what in your immediate environment may have helped trigger your current depression. Penny, for instance, believes that the move from city to retirement community—even though she looked forward to it—somehow undermined her confidence and then unleashed anxieties she didn't even know she had. "All of a sudden I had to make new friends, see myself in a different light," Penny explains, "and it frightened me. Who was I, really, if I wasn't the owner of the bookstore on Sixty-third Street? If I wasn't vice-chairman of my neighborhood association?"

Maude's son, Mike, sees something about his mother's descent into depression that she overlooked: A tenant who moved into the apartment Maude rents upstairs from her own disturbs Maude endlessly with loud music and late-night parties. For months Maude has attempted to evict the tenant but to no avail. As relatively minor as this struggle may seem, Mike thinks it has undermined his normally strong-willed mother. "She's helped her children and grandchildren through I don't know how many crises in the last few years, and she's faced her own medical problems with such courage," he says. "She even seemed to take my father's death in stride, coming out the other side of her grief with her same tough-nugget kind of spirit. But this thing with her tenant . . . I think that, coupled with the undeniable fact that she's getting older and feeling more run-down in general, just put her over the edge."

Nick, on the other hand, wants to concentrate on his physical health and his fears about losing independence and agility as his arthritis progresses. He believes that if he regains some sense of control over the disease by participating in physical therapy and working with his doctor on finding the right medication, the symptoms of depression may lift.

Is there a stressful situation or relationship in your life that might exacerbate your depression? Did a relationship you value end recently, or do you have unresolved feelings of guilt or anger about a particular relationship? Were you or someone you love recently diagnosed with an illness? These factors might be obvious to you or, as they were for Maude and Nick, hidden beneath layers of self-doubt and confusion.

To identify and change self-defeating thought patterns and behaviors: If you're like most people who suffer with depression, you've made a kind of internal audiotape of self-criticism and pessimistic thoughts. You play it back every time you try to start to enjoy a favorite hobby or begin a new project or make a vow to get back into the social swing of things. The tape might say "You were never good at knitting anyway, why bother?" or "Remember the last time you made a proposal to your boss? He turned you down flat. You're just too old to make a difference in the corporation now," or "What's the point in going to the party? You never have a good time anyway." One of the most important goals of therapy is to erase this tape and make a new one filled with more positive, self-affirming thoughts.

"My negative self-tape is about sixty-three years old," Janet confesses. "Maybe because I grew up in a household where we didn't talk about my mother's mental illness, I never felt comfortable with who I was or what I was feeling. I couldn't do anything right in my mother's eyes, and my father . . . well, he just couldn't cope with either of us. I'm now the poster girl for 'I can't,' 'I shouldn't,' 'I'll never make it.' I'm really working hard to look at my goals and my abilities—my dreams about my life—with a little more realism and a little less negativity."

To learn to set realistic goals: If you're like most people in the midst of a depression, your life right now looks out of control. You feel overwhelmed just by the laundry piled up in the closet or the unpaid bills stuffed in the kitchen drawer, to say nothing of making plans for your retirement or taking the grandchildren for the vacation that you promised them. A therapist can help you set priorities and break down larger tasks into smaller more manageable ones until slowly you reduce what currently might seem like a mountain of unmet obligations.

To identify sources of support and ask for help: We've said it before, but it bears repeating: Depression is one of the most isolating of all chronic illnesses. It's likely that you've shut yourself off from friends and loved ones as you've struggled, alone, with your feelings. With help from your therapist, you can identify the people in your life you most want to connect with again and learn to ask for their support in direct, appropriate ways.

Choosing a Therapist

As you may remember from Chapter 3, there are several different types of mental health professionals who can help you work through your depression and toward the goals we have discussed. Most likely you'll choose either a psychiatrist (a medical doctor with special training in mental health), a psychologist (someone with a doctoral degree in psychology and clinical experience in treating mental and emotional illness), or a licensed social worker who specializes in psychotherapy. Psychiatric nurses, pastoral counselors, alcohol counselors, and other types of therapists are also available.

How should you decide what type of therapist to choose? And what individual among that group might be right for you? These days it's probably wise to start by checking with your medical insurance or health plan to see if it covers mental health services and, if so, how you can obtain these benefits. As mentioned in Chapter 3, many policies have arbitrary limits and may cover only 50 percent of the costs of a fixed number of visits per year. If you're one of the increasing numbers of Americans who are members of health maintenance organizations, for instance, you may be limited in your freedom to choose who can treat you and how long you are to be treated. Medicare has particularly strict regulations.

If you have some discretionary income and are not on Medicare, you may want to seek care with your own funds if you are able. The advantage of paying for care yourself is that you will not have restrictions on how many sessions you may have or what therapist you visit. Most therapists of all types see people in private practice outside HMOs. They will usually accept insurance as payment or part payment and make a fee arrangement with you.

Once you know from what pool of therapist you can draw, you might want to ask your primary care physician for suggestions on who among them might be right for you. Ask for several referrals as well as a copy of your medical records so that the therapist has them to examine at your first appointment. If you need further referrals, your local medical or psychiatric society (see the Resource Guide, page 252), community mental health center, and medical school are also good sources. You should feel free to specify the age, sex, race, or religious background of the therapist if any of those factors is important to you.

Select two or three therapists, and phone for information about appointment availability, location, and cost of the first visit. At your first appointment, ask about fees, appointment flexibility, cancellation policy, and insurance form procedures or HMO copayment policies. Most important, ask the therapist how much experience she or he has in treating depression, what kinds of approaches he or she feels most comfortable using (we discuss those approaches later in the chapter), and how many sessions she or he usually suggests to treat depression.

After your initial session, think about how you felt with the therapist. Did you feel he or she listened to you and had a sense of your pain and your problems? Did you think you could trust him or her? Did you feel relatively at ease talking about your problems? Did the therapist take time to understand your particular medical problems and to explain how physical illnesses you have might be influencing the course of your depression?

Only if you believe you can establish a trusting, comfortable relationship (called the therapeutic alliance)—one that allows you to reveal your innermost feelings to an accepting and supportive professional—should you agree to continue with the therapist. Keep in mind that it may take time for such a solid relationship to develop, but you should believe from the start that the potential exists. Please note that if you feel uncomfortable or dissatisfied with either the relationship or your progress at any point during therapy, you should not hesitate to talk to the therapist about it and, if you still feel uncomfortable, to change therapists.

Once you choose a therapist you think might work for you, you're ready to start the hard but rewarding work of sorting through the emotional and practical problems underlying and complicating your depression. There are several different ways to approach this task, and we describe them here.

Understanding Therapeutic Approaches

Most mental health professionals today are trained in a variety of psychotherapeutic techniques. The person you choose will probably tailor his or her approach to your particular problem, personality, and needs. He or she will make a careful assessment of your current problem, including the circumstances that may have led to your depression, and your past history, family history, and medical history. The therapist will then recommend a course of treatment appropriate for you. It may involve some combination of individual, family, and group therapy as well as medication (which must be prescribed by a psychiatrist or other medical doctor).

Individual Therapy

In most cases of depression, you'll benefit most by working with a therapist one-on-one. If you start with individual therapy (and you probably will), it may include one or a combination of the following:

Psychodynamic psychotherapy

Psychodynamic therapy is based on the premise that current difficulties are often the result of unresolved past conflicts. Like its older and more complex cousin Freudian psychoanalysis, psychodynamic psychotherapy brings past conflicts into present awareness, thereby helping the patient understand and deal with them in an appropriate manner.

If your therapist chooses this approach, she or he will encourage you to talk about past experiences and see what impact they might have on your current situation. The therapist will act as a guide to building greater self-awareness and understanding. This will allow you to gain some measure of control over your life and, one hopes, to make more positive choices in the future.

A popular type of psychodynamic psychotherapy, called brief dynamic psychotherapy, concentrates on only those issues directly related to your depression. For instance, if you believe that your symptoms stem from the recent loss of a job, the therapist will help you address both your feelings about the loss and the practical and financial aspects that are making it difficult for you to cope.

Psychodynamic psychotherapy may be brief, consisting of fewer than twenty-five weekly sessions, or long term, with one or two sessions a week over several years. Some people with chronic depression may find psychodynamic psychotherapy helpful in resolving long-standing issues, thought patterns, and behaviors. The distorted ways of thinking and coping that the therapist will try to uncover include:

Repression: This involves the stuffing down of threatening thoughts, impulses, memories, or wishes so that they remain embedded in the unconscious. Penny, for example, repressed memories of the abuse she suffered at the hands of her grandfather until she made dramatic changes in her life, moving into a retirement community from the city and retiring.

Denial: The inability to accept a painful or an unpleasant reality is often a natural step in the grief or transition process but may become problematic if it persists for too long. "I sure didn't face my wife's death head-on," Jake admits. "It paralyzed my thinking, in a way. I couldn't move, couldn't think about it, never mind start creating a new life without her. I just pretended it never happened, until the life I did have fell apart."

Rationalization: This is a way of substituting acceptable reasons for your real motivations. "I can easily convince myself that I'm staying in bed all day because taking care of my mother just wears me out," Janet says. "And then a week will go by and I'll realize that nothing's gotten done, not even things my mother needs me to do, like picking up her prescriptions. But I sure can convince myself that I need to sleep."

Intellectualization: This allows you to objectify painful feelings or situations so that they do not touch you emotionally but exist only as a kind of intellectual reference point. There are several other defense mechanisms, all used for the same reason: to keep us from coming to terms with very real but very painful realities in our past and present. Once your defense mechanisms are identified, your therapist will help you replace them with more helpful and positive coping strategies:

1. *Sublimation* involves taking an unhealthy impulse and redirecting toward a more positive and acceptable behavior.
2. *Humor* helps you cope by focusing on the ridiculous and comic aspects of life and of even the most painful situations.

3. *Mastery and control,* the ultimate signs of mental health and maturity, involve the ability to confront a difficult and painful challenge directly and without becoming overwhelmed by either your feelings or the practical aspects it entails.

Cognitive behavioral therapy

Behind this type of therapy is the idea that self-criticism and negative thinking patterns can trigger depression. In other words, it could be that your view of yourself and your place in the world controls or directs your emotions. If you constantly berate yourself, expect yourself to fail, and make negative (usually inaccurate) assessments of what others think of you, depression is sure to be the result. Such thoughts can lead to passivity, apathy, isolation, and negativistic expectations that at least exacerbate if not trigger depression. Cognitive therapy attempts to interrupt this cycle by identifying cognitive errors and instituting more positive patterns of thinking. Older men and women who benefit most from this type of therapy are motivated to change, and they also have the cognitive and psychological ability to identify the way negative thoughts contribute to their depressed mood. It helps to be willing and able to work collaboratively with the therapist, perform goal-directed tasks, and identify new ways of processing information.

If you and your therapist decide to try cognitive behavioral therapy, you'll work to reframe these negative thought patterns, to change them into realistic and reaffirming ones. You'll learn to become more aware of the thoughts and attitudes that depress you, challenge their validity, and then to replace them with more positive alternatives. The first step in this approach involves identifying the specific types of negative thoughts you harbor. Which among these dysfunctional thinking patterns do you follow?

All-or-nothing thinking: Do you think only in extremes? If you gain two pounds one week, do you see yourself as a fat slob with no willpower? If your wife dismisses your ideas for your next vacation, do you conclude you're unlovable or that your marriage is in terrible trouble?

Magnifying or minimizing: If you stub your toe getting out of bed in the morning, do you automatically conclude that your day is sure to be a bad one? If your husband pays you a compliment, do you assume it's because he wants something from you or must have done something he feels guilty about?

Personalization: How often do you relate a negative event—one that has nothing to do with you—to something about you or the way you behave? If someone tailgates you while you're driving, do you rightly lay the blame on his shoulders for being rude, or do you assume you were in the way or are just too old to drive?

Automatic thinking: If your first thoughts whenever you attempt to throw a dinner party or begin a new project are "It'll never work out" and "I know I'll screw up," you're taking part in automatic thinking that's sure to undermine your efforts.

Once you figure out what kinds of undermining thought patterns you've created, your therapist will help you restructure the patterns and refocus your behavior. One specific cognitive therapy is called cognitive rehearsal. Here you envision a challenging or troubling situation, imagine how you might meet or solve it, then break the process down into manageable steps. With help from your therapist, you rehearse each step mentally, erasing the negative thoughts—the "I can't"—and replace them with "I will" and "I can."

Cognitive behavioral therapy is relatively brief (usually sixteen to twenty sessions, sometimes up to thirty to forty sessions in patients with chronic depression) and works to address your most pressing concerns. A related type of psychotherapy is called behavioral therapy. Unfortunately many managed care plans pay for only six to twelve sessions; that makes this form of therapy out of reach for people on fixed incomes in these plans.

Behavioral therapy

As its name implies, behavioral therapy concentrates on identifying and changing negative patterns of behavior, rather than thought patterns, as is true for cognitive behavioral therapy. Behavioral therapy is especially helpful for disorders characterized by specific abnormal behavior patterns, such as substance abuse, alcoholism, and eating disorders. It also seems to help elderly people, who may have ingrained patterns of behavior that require "undoing" in order for them to cope successfully with their current challenges.

If you decide to participate in behavioral therapy, the therapist will give you "homework assignments"—specific tasks you must accomplish by the next therapy session—encourage you to succeed, and monitor your progress. There are several techniques that he or she might use to help you change your negative patterns into more positive ones.

Behavior modification: This attempts to reward good behaviors while discouraging negative ones in an effort to break undermining patterns. Your therapist might encourage you to treat yourself to a manicure (or another pleasurable activity), for instance, every time you manage to keep a date with a friend or finish an assignment at work on time.

Daily mood monitoring: Daily mood monitoring is often one of the first interventions utilized. If your therapist decides to use this method for treatment, he or she will ask you to track your moods, rating your level of depression from one to ten every day while noting one or two reasons why you think you feel the way you do. This will help identify stressors and high-light mood variability over a period of time.

The older person's pleasant events schedule: Some therapists use this tool to measure both the frequency of pleasant events and the subjective pleasure derived from them. If your therapist uses this method, he or she will ask you to keep a record of your activities, rating the amount of pleasure they gave you, over a few weeks or a month. From this information the therapist can help focus you on increasing the frequency of pleasant events while identifying activities or events that caused you to feel unhappy or stressed. For instance, if you've withdrawn from your friends, your therapist might help you schedule some time for phone calls or coffee breaks with people during the week. You'll be asked to keep those dates as if they were business appointments, even if you have negative feelings about them at first.

"It took me a while to reconnect with friends and especially acquaintances, like at the golf course," Nick admits. "I dreaded it so much, and I still don't know why. I just didn't want to see or talk to anybody. But the second time was easier than the first, and then I began to enjoy getting out and playing golf, just being with the guys. It's really helped."

Stress reduction techniques: Stress—an overused term to describe a very real set of physical, emotional, and psychological reactions to pressures of all kinds—is without question a common complicating factor in cases of depression and its common cohort anxiety at any age. Learning how to reduce the stress you feel through meditation, exercise, or even bio-feedback (methods we talk about in Chapter 8) may well help alleviate your symptoms of depression and give you a feeling of self-control and mastery. A therapist treating you with behavioral therapy can help you identify sources of stress in your life as well as guide you through some stress reduction techniques.

Interpersonal psychotherapy

According to studies by the National Institute of Mental Health, interpersonal therapy is one of the most promising types of individual therapy when it comes to treating depression. Interpersonal (ITP) therapy is usually fairly short term—normally consisting of twelve to sixteen weekly sessions—and focuses on correcting current problems in your life.

ITP therapy is based on the theory that disturbed social and personal relationships can cause or precipitate depression. In turn the illness may make these relationships or situations more problematic. If you become involved in this kind of therapy, your therapist will work to help you understand how the way you relate to others relates to your depression.

Interpersonal therapy offers distinct advantages to older people who are making difficult transitions, such as retirement, widowhood, or a move to a nursing home or an assisted-living facility. It combines features of psychodynamic and cognitive therapy, but its main focus is on the individual's social role and network of relationships. When it comes to helping older people in the midst of depression, ITP therapy is especially helpful in focusing on these common issues:

- Abnormal grief reactions
- Interpersonal role disputes
- Difficult role transitions
- Inadequate social skills, including those caused or complicated by isolation

Unlike psychoanalytic psychotherapy, interpersonal therapy does not spend a lot of time addressing unconscious phenomena, such as defense mechanisms or internal conflicts. Instead it focuses primarily on the here-and-now factors that directly interfere with your ability to cope with the practical, social, and emotional circumstances of your life.

Psychoanalysis

Established by Sigmund Freud in the early part of the twentieth century, psychoanalysis is based on the concept that depression and other mental and emotional disturbances are the result of past conflicts that people push into their unconscious. In very general terms, psychoanalysts work with patients to explore past hurts, failures, and traumas that fester within and prevent the patients from having full and satisfying lives.

In most instances psychoanalysis is not the treatment of choice for people with depression whose mental and emotional problems tend to be—at least to start—more situational and immediate in nature. The process is lengthy and intense. If you decide to undergo analysis, you'll meet with a psychiatrist three to five times a week for at least two years and often much longer. Some common psychoanalytic techniques include free association, in which you speak openly and freely about whatever comes to mind while the analyst remains neutral and relatively passive, and dream analysis, in which the analyst attempts to uncover your subconscious desires and fears as they are revealed in the dreams you remember and relate to her or him.

Although some psychoanalysts today prescribe medication as part of the therapy, especially for their depressed patients, most traditional psychoanalysts do not. The primary therapeutic tool is the relationship that forms between the analyst and patient during the intense and lengthy sessions. In addition, psychoanalysts may use free association as a way to connect you to any unresolved conflicts from your childhood that have created and perpetuated undermining patterns of behavior and thinking. One thing the analyst looks for are defense mechanisms or distorted ways of thinking about a situation that interfere with your mental and emotional health.

"Believe it or not, I'm considering going into analysis," Peter remarks. "Now that I'm through the worst of the depression, I see that there are a lot of things about my life, my childhood, my way of looking at the world and my relationships, that I don't understand. Analysis interests me in an intellectual way, I guess. I like the idea of really exploring what's inside my mind. We'll see how it goes!"

Group Therapy and Self-Help Organizations

Group therapy, the most widely used form of psychotherapy today, works toward the same general goals as individual therapy: developing a greater understanding and acceptance of yourself and learning more effective and appropriate coping strategies. As its name suggests, the process takes place in a group setting, usually among people with similar problems and life circumstances. The therapist is there to set ground rules, guide discussions, and resolve conflicts, but the bulk of the work is performed by members of the group. By interacting with one another, members can begin to identify patterns of their behavior and personality that may be interfering with healthy relationships outside the group. They challenge one another's defense mechanisms, share insights into common problems, and provide support and empathy within a safe and structured environment.

Group therapy can be especially helpful for older people because it introduces them to a group of their peers (thus becoming an antidote to isolation) in a less intimidating atmosphere than a one-on-one situation may represent. Interestingly, therapists find that elders who participate in group therapy tend to show much less competition and aggression than their younger counterparts, reflecting perhaps the maturity and perspective that come with age. Furthermore, group therapy offers opportunities for growth and change:

- Establishing a sense of identity within society, including a sexual identity
- Becoming part of a nurturing support system
- Resolving old conflicts through reflection, reminiscences, and reenactments within the context of the group
- Enhancing self-esteem by receiving encouragement and input from peers
- Adapting to and accepting losses through the experiences of others in the same situation

Group therapy gives Jake a forum to discuss not only the loss of his wife but his concerns about becoming dependent on his daughter. Hearing how others deal with those same feelings and struggles has given him a new perspective on how to cope with his own situation. Perhaps even more important, at least in the long run, is the sense of companionship and society Jake has found within the group.

"What I like best sometimes is just sitting around and gabbing about the so-called good old days," Jake says with a smile. "When I talk about my war experiences, everybody knows I'm talking about World War Two and not Vietnam!"

Group therapy, as well as its lay counterpart, the

self-help group, is not usually recommended for someone in the midst of a deep depression, when feelings of low self-esteem and low energy need more immediate, one-on-one attention. However, if the idea of meeting in a group appeals to you, talk to your doctor or current therapist about it. He or she can help place you in a group that's right for you.

Family and marriage therapy

Family therapy and marriage therapy focus not on you as an individual but you as a member of a family or marital unit. Although family or marriage therapy is usually not the first choice for people suffering with depression, it may be helpful when combined with individual therapy under certain circumstances. If your depression appears to be seriously jeopardizing your marriage, for instance, or interfering with the family dynamic or—conversely—if you think your marriage or family relationships are triggering your feelings of hopelessness and anxiety, then you and your therapist might suggest you and your spouse and/or family visit a family therapist to work through these issues.

"My depression and especially my memories of sexual abuse from childhood have been seriously affecting my marriage, and probably for a long time," Penny says. "My therapist has suggested that once we work through a few more things on our own, we bring my husband in on the process. He's got a lot of anger and feelings of rejection, I know that. We need to work them out together."

You've now had a chance to see the many different strategies used to treat depression and other disorders within a therapeutic setting. In Chapter 7 we deal in more depth with how depression affects the family.

Important Questions and Answers About Chapter 6

Q. I think I have a lot of negative behavior patterns, but I also know I have some problems in my past. Should I be looking for a therapist who practices behavior therapy or psychodynamic therapy or what?

A. At this point don't worry too much about which approach to take. It's far more important to find a therapist you trust and feel you can work with. As we said, most therapists will use a combination of approaches—a little cognitive therapy to erase negative ways of thinking, a little behavior therapy if you have trouble breaking out of unproductive behavior patterns, etc.—depending on your symptoms, your personality, and your needs. If one method doesn't work, the therapist will try another, or a variety of others, until you feel better and can cope with your challenges in more effective and healthy ways.

Q. If depression is a biological illness involving neurotransmitters and brain chemicals, why would talking about problems help relieve symptoms?

A. Psychotherapy helps treat a biological illness like depression in two ways. First, it helps people make realistic assessments of their problems, allowing them to see, perhaps for the first time, the ways that depression has undermined their personal, social, and professional lives.

Second, as emphasized in Chapter 4, the mind (our emotions and thought processes) and the brain (tissue and chemicals) are intimately linked. A fascinating study reported in the February 1995 issue of the *Archives of General Psychiatry* described an experiment that used positron-emission tomography (PET) scans—sophisticated imaging technology—to show how behavioral therapy affects biological processes. Scientists studied nine people suffering from obsessive-compulsive disorder, an anxiety disorder that compels people to perform certain acts over and over again. In these people three parts of the brain that usually act independently become hyperactive together when the compulsion takes hold.

After the patients underwent ten weeks of cognitive behavior therapy—without medication—their brain structures were less hyperactive and, most important, worked more independently of one another. As a result, the patients were less plagued by obsessive-compulsive behavior. Exactly how and why such dramatic physical changes result from changing behavior patterns remains an exciting avenue of research.

Q. I'm a seventy-year-old Hispanic woman from Central America and come from a very traditional family. Should I look for a Hispanic therapist who knows about my customs and upbringing?

A. You may feel more comfortable working with someone with a similar background, but it isn't absolutely necessary—as long the therapist is aware that cultural differences do affect the course of therapy. In November 1995 the *American Journal of Psychiatry* published guidelines for psychiatric evaluation that for the first time explicitly recommended that a therapist consider a patient's cultural or ethnic background during treatment.

One of the most fundamental cultural differences

may be in the way the patient sees the illness itself. Some disorders of the mind that we recognize in Western cultures do not exist in other societies. Anorexia nervosa, for instance, appears in modern industrialized societies but not in Native American cultures or cultures in developing nations. In Japan mental health professionals recognize a malady known as *taijin kyofuso* (fear of people), which has no correlate here in the United States. A person suffering from *taijin kyofuso* has a morbid dread of doing something that will embarrass other people. Medical anthropologists believe this disorder stems from a concept of social shame that simply has no counterpart in the United States.

As multicultural diversity becomes the rule rather than the exception, more and more mental health professionals will need to be aware of, and able to adapt therapy to, each patient's background. Many teaching institutions now offer students of psychiatry and psychology training in various cultural traditions and how to assess the cultural impact on the patients' problems and treatment strategies.

CHAPTER SEVEN

Depression and the Family

"I'm not in this alone, as much as I want to be," Dianne admits. "I don't have children, but I have siblings and nieces and nephews who depend on me or at least who relate to me as a special person in their lives. I had no idea how much this has affected them or in what ways until recently. The depression brought out their fears about my Alzheimer's, which I think they'd denied as much as they could, and they're very upset and confused. Because I've been so depressed and withdrawn, I haven't been able to help. I want so much to be a part of their lives again, a full part, so we can be a family again."

Dianne's concerns about her family and their reactions to her illness are perfectly natural and very common. Depression affects not only every aspect of someone's personal life and health but also his or her relationships with other individuals and the family dynamic in general. Indeed the line "No man is an island" may be a cliché, but it has particular resonance and meaning when it comes to the effect depression has on one's personal life and social structure.

While your way of relating to the world changes as

a side effect of the disease, it's important that you understand that your spouse and family members too will experience change in the ways that they relate not only to you but often to each other as well. Furthermore, and just as important, you should be aware that depression is often a contagious disease and can be every bit as infectious as a flu or cold virus. More than 25 percent of family members and 50 percent of spouses of depressed people end up requiring treatment for depression themselves. The danger of "catching" depression is especially keen for the person who acts as the primary caregiver to the older person with depression, usually the spouse or an adult child. Because depression in late life is often accompanied by another chronic illness, the burden on the caregiver may be quite heavy.

In the first half of this chapter we discuss some of the difficult adjustments families must make when a member falls victim to depression and how you can work together with your family to avoid the common pitfalls. We devote the second half of the chapter to the caregiver and the special attention he or she deserves and in fact requires in order to stay healthy.

Protecting the Family Circle

"All happy families resemble one another; every unhappy family is unhappy in its own way," writes Leo Tolstoy in his novel *Anna Karenina*. As you no doubt have already discovered, the diagnosis of depression—or any other chronic illness, for that matter—can throw an entire family for an emotional loop, no matter which member it strikes or who becomes the primary caregiver. It is impossible to generalize about the kinds of effects such disruption will cause in a family since that aspect of depression is as individualized and particular as all others.

One type of dysfunction that often occurs in families when depression (or any other illness strikes) is called the social breakdown syndrome. The term refers to the disruption in the family structure when one member no longer is able to fill his or her social role in the family. If it's a parent who becomes depressed, children (even adult children) temporarily lose the person at the center of their family, the one who dispenses advice and comfort, the person they could count on to put their needs first.

"My mother, as irascible as she's always been, is also my best friend—next to my wife, that is," Maude's son, Mike, explains. "She's been sick in the past, but nothing really scared me until this depression. She just wasn't herself, and that means she couldn't be the same friend to me. I'm nearly fifty, but I felt abandoned, angry, not only at her but at my sister, who wasn't there to experience any of it because she lives three thousand miles away. I didn't even realize I resented, even a little bit, having to take so much responsibility for my mother. I even found myself getting angry at my dad, who's been dead for ten years. My mother's depression brought up as much stuff in my psyche as it did in hers, I think!"

TEN WORST THINGS TO SAY
TO SOMEONE DEPRESSED

1. No one ever said life was fair.
2. I thought you were stronger than that.
3. Pull yourself up by your bootstraps.
4. These should be the most fulfilling years of your life.
5. Happiness is a choice.
6. You can do anything you want to if you just set your mind to it.
7. You have no reason to feel this way, you have such a good life.
8. All you need is a hobby, something to keep you busy.
9. It can't be *that* bad.
10. Just don't dwell on yourself so much.

TEN BEST THINGS TO SAY
TO SOMEONE DEPRESSED

1. I care what's happening to you.
2. You're not alone in this.
3. Do you want a hug?
4. You are not crazy.
5. I'm sorry you're in so much pain.
6. I don't know exactly what you're feeling, but I'm here for you.
7. I value your friendship.
8. What can I do to help?

9. Don't be afraid. You'll find the help you need, and I'll help you find it.
10. Take your time getting better. There's no hurry.

Depression is also likely to have a trickle-down effect on families, affecting not only the immediate family but the extended one as well. "All the attention I'm paying to my father, and all the worry I'm feeling, really get in the way of my relationship with my boyfriend," Julie remarks. "I didn't realize how distant I've become and how my problems now are interfering with our lives. My boyfriend has kids from a previous marriage and we'd become very close. They feel abandoned by me because of all the time I'm spending with my dad. It gets so complicated."

In a way the exact role the parent plays or the closeness of the relationship between the parent and child doesn't matter. Maude's depression, and the issues about her health and her future that the illness brought up, threw Mike's sister, Margaret, for an emotional loop even though she and her mother have been estranged for many years.

"I think it's even harder for Margaret in some ways," Mike explains. "Her first reaction was one of terrible guilt; she thought that somehow the problems they had together triggered the depression somehow. But really, it's actually a good thing in a way because Margaret now realizes she doesn't want my mother to die before they've had a chance to reconcile. That's something positive anyway."

Depression also has a profound effect on the relationship between partners. When depression occurs in late life, other issues, such as retirement and chronic illness, may complicate the marriage at the same time. In addition, the primary side effects of the disease—isolation and loneliness—often spill over into the partner's universe. Both spouses are likely to have difficulty sustaining friendships with people outside the family circle, while the well spouse is also under considerable strain to keep the family itself functioning as normally as possible on his or her own.

"What's been hard on my wife, Shannon, is my lack of interest, or rather near terror of being in social situations," Peter says. "Because of our age difference—I'm nearly twenty years older than she—we've always had a little difficulty working out a social life that satisfies both of us. We'd made a lot of progress, but since I've been depressed and haven't wanted to go out or entertain, Shannon's felt lonely and trapped too, almost as lonely and trapped as I have."

In addition to disrupting outside relationships, depression can seriously undermine intimacy between partners. Often the well partner feels rejected or or abandoned by the depressed loved one physically, emotionally, and sexually.

"I said to my husband right out loud, 'I don't love you anymore,' " Penny says. "It was horrible, but that's the way I felt. If he'd walked out the door, I wouldn't have blamed him. Instead he looked at me, took my hand, and said, 'Penny, that's just the depression talking. We'll get through this, I promise.' That meant more to me than I can say. It's the only way I've been able to hang on."

Isolation, loneliness, fear, worry: These are just a few of the emotions that crop up when one family member experiences a disease like depression. Here are some other common reactions:

Frustration: "I felt ridiculous even thinking it," Nick's wife, Angela, admits, "but I could just strangle Nick sometimes! His moping, his unhappiness. I know it isn't fair to him, I know he has an illness, and I try so hard to be patient. But sometimes I just snap."

Anxiety: "I'm scared, there's no doubt about that," Jake's daughter, Julie, says. "I wake up at night worried sick about my father, if he's going to get well, what will happen if he doesn't. I'm not eating right either. I know I have to get a handle on all this—and about my own feelings about my mother's death—or I won't be able to help him."

Guilt: Partners and family members often feel guilty when someone they love becomes depressed, and for two different reasons. Some feel guilty because they believe that in some way they may have triggered the depression. That's the case with Maude's daughter, Margaret. Others harbor guilt about being well while their loved one suffers, a different two-prong guilt: that they might have caused it in some way and that they are well.

Anger and resentment: "After dealing with my mother's illness for so long, all my life really, you'd think I would have looked for signs of resentment and frustration in my own kids," Janet remarks, "but I missed it. Too deep in my own problems, I guess. Then my daughter let loose about a month ago when she came home and found me in bed at three in the afternoon. Yelling at me for being lazy, for not being there for her, for being self-indulgent. It seemed to come out of nowhere, but now I realize how long it must have been building up for her. After all, I've experienced periods of depression throughout her whole life too. We're now in therapy together, working out all this anger and resentment floating around in this family.''

Just by reading the list and description of emotions a family member's depression can generate, you can see how easy it might be for a spouse or child to become depressed as a result. But as is true for so much about depression (indeed about most difficult challenges), knowledge is power. The more you and your family know about depression and its potential effects on the family dynamic, the more you'll be able to cope with the challenges that lie ahead.

"What I didn't realize," Nick explains, "is the effect my low mood and tendency to withdraw was having on my young grandchild. Jeremy's only four years old, so I didn't think I needed to talk with him about my illness at all. But he started misbehaving, throwing temper tantrums, sulking. It was my wife who finally talked about what was going on. Part of it was the fact that he and his family recently moved to be closer to me, but most of it was my behavior toward him. He just looked up at my wife and said, 'What's wrong with Grandpa?' and burst into tears. So she, my daughter-in-law, and I sat down and explained that I wasn't feeling well and needed a little time to get better. I think it helped him adjust better.''

Indeed it is extremely important that you explain your symptoms of depression—all of them, even those you think no one will notice—to the people closest to you. This is particularly important with a disease like depression, which often involves periods of crying, mood swings, and irritability that many family members—especially young children—may otherwise take personally.

Understanding Family Therapy

"I've got a forty-nine-year-old wife, a ten-year-old son, two grown daughters, and now a grandchild," Peter remarks with a chuckle. "Even though I'm considering undergoing analysis, I thought I'd better get us into some family therapy to work out the issues and stresses my depression brought to the surface."

Many families like Peter's find family therapy helpful in learning to cope with the extra pressures and stresses depression places on the family. As Dianne noticed, a disease like depression often brings up issues and fears long buried within the family history and context. A therapist trained in working with families to resolve problems and conflicts can help uncover, identify, and manage them.

There are many different approaches to family therapy. Some emphasize problem solving and tend to be brief and focused. Despite Maude's reluctance to seek therapy, Mike finally convinced her to join him and his family in therapy to work out the issues surrounding their moving into her home. It took several sessions, but now they all feel more comfortable about meeting the challenges to come with less stress and dissension. In other cases family therapy is more exploratory and insight-oriented. That can be helpful in families like Janet's, where long-standing and problematic ways of interacting and behaving exist.

In working with couples and families, therapists look beyond an individual's feelings or behavior to the impact these feelings and behaviors have on others. The method they use is called systems orientation. It looks at the family as a unit that works (or fails to work) together, with an understanding that all couples and families have both strengths and vulnerabilities that surface under stress and that each member's behavior and feelings impact on those of the others.

Among the principles of system orientation therapists use to identify the problems within the family are:

Context: As you probably have discovered already, your struggle with depression probably affects your spouse, children, and close family or friends. In turn their reactions may create more stress and anxiety for you, which could well exacerbate your disease. A therapist can help you identify the pattern of these relationships and see if there are better ways to manage them.

Interaction: The way you and your family communicate with one another is just as important as the content of what you say and do. In family therapy you can learn new and more satisfying ways of relating to one another.

Fit: What is "normal" in one family isn't necessarily so in another. "One of the things I found out, even at this late age," Peter explains, "is that my wife has a completely different idea of how a family should interact. She's shocked at how close my kids are to me, how easily they yell and criticize—with love, of course. She and her family are much more reserved and not used to talking about their feelings. I think that put some stress on our marriage, especially as I withdrew into depression and left her to deal with the kids.''

Adaptability: Are you and your family as a unit able to ''go with the flow'' of changing circumstances? Or is your household either too disorganized and chaotic or too rigid and inflexible to adapt quickly and smoothly? A therapist can help your family develop more effective strategies for facing challenges together and separately so that the overall stress level is lower.

Cohesion: Cohesion refers to the relative connectedness and separateness in a couple or family. Does each member of your family tend to act independently and thus find it difficult to come together as a unit to face a crisis like your depression? Family therapy can help your family to acknowledge your interdependence, provide mutual support to one another, and work cooperatively to reach individual and family goals.

Just for Caregivers

Caring for someone with an illness like depression is a tough job, one that can be every bit as draining as the depression itself. Unfortunately the needs of the caregiver all too often become lost as the focus of attention remains on the depressed person through the course of the disease.

Are you a caregiver to someone with depression or other chronic illness? If so, filling out this worksheet may help you understand your feelings and priorities as well as assess your risk for developing depression or other illness yourself.

CAREGIVER SANITY WORKSHEET

The most *stressful* thing about caring for someone who is depressed is_____.

The most *irritating* thing about caring someone who is depressed is_____.

The most *exhausting* thing about caring for someone who is depressed is_____.

The most *rewarding* thing about caring for someone who is depressed is_____.

The most *frightening* thing about caring for someone who is depressed is_____.

Once you've finished the above statements, talk over your feelings with a trusted friend or therapist. The process of recognition and expression alone will help you better manage your stress and anxiety.

Answer the following questions yes or no.

Do you get five to six hours of uninterrupted sleep most nights?   _____

Can you arrange to be alone for some
portion of every day?   _____

Is there someone you could/would call
for help at 2:00 A.M.?   _____

Is there one friend or family member
who could/would loan you money if
you needed it?   _____

Is there anyone in your life who fully
    understands your day-to-day
    stresses?   _____

If you answered more than one or two of these questions with a no, you may be at risk for developing
depression or another illness even as you attempt to
help the one you love recover. You may be able to
avoid that risk if you follow these tips:

- *Accept your frustration—and voice it.*

Keeping your emotions bottled up in order to spare
your loved one with depression may only end up
backfiring. In the end it's likely you'll only become
more and more stressed, irritable, and unhappy.

- *Be assertive.*

Make sure that your opinions and needs are heard by
your loved one and, if appropriate, his or her doctor or
therapist. It's far too easy for your own concerns to
become lost in the struggle to treat your partner or
parent's depression.

- *Take care of yourself first.*

Unless you are physically and mentally fit, you can't
take care of anyone else, and you'll have trouble
maintaining healthy relationships of all kinds, including the one you have with the person you're attempting to nurse. That means getting enough sleep, eating

well, exercising on a regular basis, and taking plenty of time out to shop, go to movies, and participate in hobbies you've always enjoyed.

- *Avoid isolating yourself from your family and friends.*

As we've said, depression is a very isolating illness for both the person who suffers from it and his or her primary caregiver.

- *Realize that you're not alone.*

There is help out there for you, not only from social service and health agencies but from your siblings, children, spouse, and friends as well. Often all you need to do is ask. (In the Resource Guide, page 252, you'll find a listing of caregiver groups across the country you can contact for more information and advice.)

In the next chapter we provide you and your loved ones with some valuable tools to help you through the recovery period and beyond. Combined with therapy and/or medication, these coping strategies will help you make it through to the other side of depression as easily as possible.

Important Questions and Answers About Chapter 7

Q. My older brother, who's just turned sixty-six, told me he's depressed and just starting medication. We've never been close, but I've never seen him so sad and withdrawn, and I'm worried. I don't even know how to start talking to him, or what to say. I don't want to say the wrong thing and alienate him. Can you help?

A. First of all, relax a little. The more anxious you are, the harder it will be for the two of you to communicate. Second, remember that the illness adds another dimension to an already very long and thus complex relationship. If you and your brother had trouble communicating before, it stands to reason that his depression may make it even more difficult. You may want to consider talking to a therapist, alone or together, to help work out some of the issues behind your estrangement.

That said, here are a few tips that may help you feel more comfortable talking to your brother about his illness:

Accept his feelings. A perfectly natural but unfortunately often counterproductive approach to helping someone with depression is to help him "count his blessings." You may be tempted, for instance, to point out what a great job your brother has, or how lucky he is to have a loving family. Although you mean well by doing so, you end up trivializing his very real feelings of despair and thus may make him feel more alone and more isolated. Instead, simply listen and accept what he tells you about his emotions and perceptions.

Express empathy. Telling your brother that you understand how hopeless and disappointing life can seem at times may help him to express his own feelings of despair without fear of being judged or dismissed.

Respect his privacy—and be patient. There's a fine line between providing loving support and hovering with anxiety and fear. Tell your brother that you love him and be available to help—just to listen if that's what he needs—but try not to appear excessively worried, which will only add to his own anxiety. Depression can take some time to resolve, even with medication and psychotherapy, and let your brother know that you understand the process and will help him through it no matter how long it takes.

Accept your limitations. You can't pull your brother out of this depression any more than you—or any one person or event—were responsible for its development. You may never be able to help him figure out "why" he's depressed and there's certainly no one thing that will snap him out of it. On the other hand, this illness may provide you with an opportunity to get to know your brother better, and to build bridges of communication and empathy that will span the rest of your lives.

Q. My wife has had Parkinson's disease for fifteen years, and it's starting to get pretty bad. I have to help her dress and eat and can't leave her alone for more than an hour or two at the most. I'm tired all the time, but I can't sleep at night. I want to laugh with her and enjoy the things we can still enjoy, but I feel flat and empty. What can I do to snap back?

A. First, realize that you're carrying a heavy load, and have been carrying that load for a long time. It's natural that you're exhausted not only from your chores but from the worry you must be feeling about the future. Second, your symptoms indicate that you may be depressed and thus require some medical attention yourself. Talk to your doctor as soon as you can. It's likely that you'll benefit from medication, therapy, or a combination of both. Remember: You'll be no good to your wife if you're ill yourself.

Third, you need to get some help in caring for your wife—you simply can't do it all yourself. Discuss home care options with your wife's doctor, and reach out as much as you can to friends and relatives for help. Find out if there's a support group for Parkinson's disease patients and their families nearby. These groups can offer a great deal of emotional support and practical advice—both of which are invaluable to you and your wife, especially as the disease progresses.

CHAPTER EIGHT

Coping Strategies
for Today and Tomorrow

"I know it sounds silly, but the best thing for me was to get back to the golf course," Nick says. "I'd shut myself off so much, not only from the guys I play with but from the sheer enjoyment of hitting a good stroke, the feel of the air, the color of the grass, the heft of the clubs on my back. I guess I look at the game—or at least why I play the game—a little differently now that I'm on the other side of this."

"For me, it was the sleep, no question about it," Penny comments. "I'd been wound up so tight, too afraid of my nightmares to want to fall asleep at night, too sad and guilty to let myself enjoy a nap during the day, even when I was exhausted. Once the medication kicked in—and the therapy, no doubt—I could finally sleep, really sleep. I cannot tell you how much better I felt, how much more manageable my life seemed."

Reading about Nick's and Penny's coping strategies probably gives you the idea that like all other aspects of depression, the recovery process is highly individualized. No two people with depression take the same path through to, as Nick puts it, "the other side." In this chapter we provide you with some valuable tools that may help you through your recovery period. Combined with medication and therapy, these coping strategies will help you make it through to the other side of your own personal cloud of depression and despair. In the sections that follow, you'll find a variety of suggestions about day-to-day living and future planning that have proved helpful to others like you who have worked successfully through depression.

In fact, more than any other chapter in this book, the material we offer here is meant for you to take or leave as you like. There are no hard-and-fast rules, no prescriptions, few statistics, only recommendations and offerings. Keep in mind that one of the keys to recovering from depression is to avoid adding any stress to your life. If you think of the suggestions here as just a long list of To Do's, you're apt to feel overwhelmed. Don't. Take your time with this chapter. Look at only one or two suggestions each day, or simply check off the ones that appeal to you and ignore the rest. Talk to your therapist about the changes you'd like to make in your daily life, and gain his or her insight on how you best can accomplish them—with or without using the advice we offer here.

Coping with Symptoms of Depression

As you've seen through the stories of the people you met throughout this book, the symptoms of depression tend to keep individuals who suffer its burdens from moving forward in their own lives as well as to isolate them from the rest of the world. The following suggestions might help you get to know yourself again and make the process of reentry into health and vitality a little easier for you.

- *Erase the negative tapes you play inside your head.*

Don't allow yourself to say "I can't" or "What's the use?" until you evaluate your situation with objectivity. Try to look for the positive aspects of your behavior and of your circumstances. Psychologist Jay Cleve, who wrote a terrific guidebook for coping with symptoms of depression called *Out of the Blues,* refers to the "inner saboteur" that exists inside each of us and comes out in full force during a depression. This saboteur judges and criticizes your behavior, denies you the ability to recognize your accomplishments, and keeps you from proceeding with new plans and activities with any hope or confidence of success. It's important to hear this voice, recognize it as negative, and replace it with a more positive, life-affirming one.

- *Avoid making major life decisions.*

Needless to say, the midst of a depression is no time for you to be making a major career change or moving to a new city or deciding to start or end a relationship. First, your judgment is not the best right now; your emotional problems keep you from seeing your strengths and true desires with any clarity. Second, making decisions is a stressful activity, one you should—if at all possible—put off until you feel better. Otherwise you risk undermining your progress.

- *Be kind to yourself.*

Stop finding fault with everything about yourself and start treating yourself well. Treat yourself to simple pleasures: Brew a cup of your favorite tea and sip it outside in the sun; read a trashy romance novel without harboring a trace of guilt about "wasting time," buy yourself a couple of tickets to the next baseball game and take a buddy. Treating yourself well doesn't have to cost money or involve abrogating your responsibilities. Simply take the time to applaud a goal you've met, a decision you've made, a good day you've spent, with something that makes you smile.

- *Give yourself time.*

If you've started your medication or psychotherapy, you probably already feel a bit better. But don't let this resurgence of energy fool you. You may not be ready to take on new responsibilities or even assume all your previous ones.

"I thought, 'Well, I'll just make myself snap out of it,' " Maude says. "I'll just put a plan of action into effect and everything'll be okay. I hired a new lawyer to help me get my tenant out, I decided to be the one to host next month's bridge games, and I even signed up to take a yoga class down at the senior center. I held it together for about two weeks, and then I could feel myself start to slip. I hate it that I'm like this, but I guess I'd better accept it. Now I'm taking my time."

You too may want to slow down your recovery process a bit, evaluate your situation carefully, then slowly begin the process of repair and rebuilding.

That's why it's especially useful to work with a therapist who can help you recognize your limitations and set realistic goals.

- *Learn to set priorities.*

Right now you may very well be overwhelmed by the tasks before you. Depending on how severe and long-standing your depression is, you may have financial problems caused by your withdrawal, your housekeeping skills may have created some organization problems, or your social life may be in serious need of repair. Working with a therapist, or with a trusted friend, figure out what aspects of your life you'd like to tackle first.

- *Add some structure to your day.*

Many people with depression find that having a schedule, one that has some continuity and regularity day to day, can be extremely helpful. It can be as simple as (1) make breakfast; (2) shower; (3) go for a walk; (4) call a friend; (5) make a shopping list for dinner; (6) go to the store; etc.

"That's what helped me most," Jake explains. "I'd been in the army so long that when I retired and didn't have any structure at all to my day, I guess I panicked. My doctor helped me plug some tasks and goals into the empty calendar. It really helps keep me focused."

Once you feel comfortable and more in control, you can make the same list, but put some time limits to each activity so that you can get the most out of your day. Every time you finish a task, cross it off your list.

Every time you do, your self-esteem will get a healthy little boost.

• *Schedule time to be with the people you love.*

If you're like most people with depression, you've shut yourself off from the people in your life. You may have done so because you didn't want to burden them with your feelings of unhappiness or despair, or you may simply lack the energy to communicate. Once you start to feel a little better, though, it's important to start bridging any gaps between yourself and your friends and family.

"I realized that not only was my husband worried about me and my health but he was worried about *us,*" Penny recalls. "We'd been sharing our whole lives for almost thirty years, but when the depression hit, and the bad memories started to flood my brain, I withdrew completely, both sexually and as his friend. My therapist helped me see how abandoned and lonely he felt—and still feels to some extent—and how I had to find ways to bring him back into my world. Now I make sure that we spend some time every day doing the things we used to do, simple things like taking a walk or cooking a meal together. I even leave him little notes in his briefcase reassuring him of my love. At first I thought it was kind of stupid, these little things, but it makes both of us feel better and more connected."

Like Penny, you'll probably want to start small. Make a breakfast date with a good friend; organize a picnic just for you and your spouse; rent a movie and

watch it with your grandkids. Work with your therapist on finding ways to heal any relationship breaches.

- *Try to identify what makes you happy and find
  ways to bring those people or activities back into
  your life.*

What often gets lost in depression is what in your
heart of hearts satisfies you and brings you pleasure.
You may have told yourself that your desires are petty
or unimportant or that you simply don't deserve to be
happy. This is negative thinking at its most undermining and will lead only to further feelings of hopelessness and despair. If you love to read fiction, don't tell
yourself it's a "waste of time." Instead join a book
group with others who share your passion so that
you'll have some support.

- *Ask trusted others for positive feedback.*

As you begin to set priorities and make plans, it might
be helpful for you to have a kind of feedback system
set up to monitor your progress and encourage you
along the way.

"I got my friend Liz to help me," Janet recalls.
"She's always there to pick me up if I fail or think
I'm failing. It's not that she's just a cheerleader or a
yes-man, but she's willing to help me see things in a
more positive light whenever possible. When I decided to stop working on a novel to take a course at
the extension school, she didn't criticize me. Instead
she let me know that I had made a good decision, that
my priorities were the right ones for me at the time. It

made a big difference. It kept me from telling myself I was too stupid or too lazy or too . . . depressed to succeed!''

If you follow the tips just listed—one or two at a time, and only the ones you think will help you through the recovery process—you'll soon find yourself back in the company of the world and perhaps even ready to tackle the next stage of life with gusto. The key to success, however, involves providing your body and mind with the raw ingredients they need to survive and thrive.

Understand Your Challenges

''I know that my deepest anxieties stemmed from not identifying the real challenges ahead of me,'' Dianne says. ''Not meeting those challenges, not even making a *plan* to meet them, just identifying them, putting them out there where I could see them.''

If you or someone you love is entering late life, there are some basic goals for development that will help you or that person accept and enjoy the changes that come with this stage of life. They include:

Making decisions about living arrangements: ''Both of us are healthy now,'' Penny says, ''but we won't always be. We've moved here, to a retirement community, but I never asked how far this place will take us. What if John has a stroke and needs long-term care? I think those issues have been eating away at me, without my even knowing. Now I've begun to ask some questions, and John and I are making concrete plans. It really has eased the stress.''

Do you know how you'd like your life to be should

you become unable to care for yourself on your own? Have you made plans with your spouse or your children? If not, consider how much less stress you'd feel if you had some control over your future living situation. As soon as you feel ready, talk to your therapist, your lawyer, your children about this issue.

Maintaining important interpersonal relationships: We've said it often throughout this book, but it bears repeating again: Loneliness undermines your physical, mental, and emotional life just as thoroughly as any disease. Find ways to bring the people you love into your world and hold them there.

Maintaining your good health, and monitoring your health care priorities: Getting older does not mean inevitable disability, but it does mean that you're likely to be faced with more and more medical challenges as the years pass. Your best strategy for staying as healthy as possible for as long as possible is to receive medical attention on a regular basis, follow your doctor's suggestions about medication and lifestyle changes, and monitor your own symptoms and side effects carefully.

"So I finally get through, or almost through, this depression, and now my doctor tells me I've got high blood pressure," Jake remarks. "He puts me on this medication, and right away I notice I'm not myself. I don't feel like eating, and I'm constipated. Before, I guess I would have figured that was just getting old. Now I go back to the doctor, explain what's going on, he puts me on another drug, and I feel better almost right away."

Indeed the first step in maintaining your good health as you age is maintaining *control* over it. The symptoms of depression no doubt took away your sense of control. As you regain your mental health through therapy, medication, or both, you'll be able to take that control right back.

Living Well

The clichés are endless: "You are what you eat," "A healthy body in a healthy mind," to name just two. In this instance, though, the clichés have important merit: If you don't treat your body with care, your mind and your emotions will undoubtedly suffer. Here are a few tips to help you get your physical life under control.

Sleep well

As you may remember from Chapters 2 and 4, sleep problems are often the first and most serious symptom of depression—and they are *not* a normal side effect of the aging process. Although sleep patterns change, you should be able to sleep deeply and wake feeling rested at every age. Without question, the less sleep you get, and the less regularly you get it, the more likely you are to suffer from mood-related disorders. The key is to establish a regular sleeping schedule. Follow these tips if you have trouble sleeping:

- *Exercise regularly.*

Physical activity both reduces stress and relaxes your muscles. However, try not to exercise in the evening, when activity may act as a stimulant. Again, age should not be a barrier to regular exercise. Ask your doctor for advice, especially if you have medical problems.

- *Set regular bedtimes.*

Try to go to bed and get up at set times every day and night. Even if you've had a bad night's sleep, get yourself out of bed at your regular time, and then try as hard as you can to stay up until your regular bedtime. If you have to drag yourself through one or two days, it's likely you'll eventually synchronize your body clock so that you'll fall asleep when you're tired and get up feeling refreshed.

- *Drink a glass of warm milk.*

Sometimes the oldest cures are also the most effective. If you can't seem to fall asleep, try drinking a glass of warm milk about a half hour before going to bed. Milk includes high levels of tryptophan, an amino acid that is the precursor of melatonin (the hormone that scientists believe ''sets'' the body's internal clock).

- *Start keeping a diary.*

Many people with depression find the dark quiet of night the perfect time to brood on their problems and dwell on their shortcomings. If you write down your fears and worries before you go to bed, you may find yourself feeling less stressed and anxious when it's time to sleep.

Eat well

Food not only is nourishment that provides your body with the raw materials it needs to function but should also be a source of pleasure. Unfortunately too many older people lose interest in food, perhaps because arthritis or other chronic illnesses make it difficult to shop and cook, perhaps because their taste buds no longer seem as acute. Depression itself often takes away the appetite, making eating seem like just one more unbearable burden. Another problem is that many people, perhaps more women than men, are actually afraid of food, of its calories, fat content, of the potential carcinogens it harbors. "On top of everything else," Penny says, "I sure didn't want to get fat. I found myself gorging anyway, on so-called low-fat food, and put on weight anyway. And I didn't even taste the food I was eating."

In Chapter 2 we cited several reasons that might cause a lack of appetite in an older man or woman. Although depression often causes a decrease in appetite, it's important that you consider these other possibilities and discuss the matter with your doctor:

- An undiscovered illness or infection
- Certain medications
- Missing or decaying teeth
- Poorly fitting dentures
- Arthritis or other disability that prohibits or limits cooking
- Alcohol abuse
- Memory lapses that interfere with eating regularly
- Lack of transportation to grocery store
- Lack of money to pay for groceries

In addition to learning the basics of a healthy diet, you should strive to take the time to enjoy the sensual aspects of eating. Smell the food as it cooks, feel its textures as you chew, savor its flavors. At least once in a while, plan special meals for yourself and your family, times when you can enjoy the pleasures of conversation along with your food.

A word of warning: People prone to depression all too often use alcohol as a form of self-medication, and an ultimately undermining form it is at that since it acts as a depressant on the central nervous system. While you're depressed, it is probably wise to avoid alcohol altogether. But once you're feeling better, and as long as you don't have an addiction to alcohol, you should feel free to enjoy a glass of wine or an occasional drink.

Exercise regularly

The benefits of physical activity are almost too numerous to mention. In addition to reducing your risk of developing heart disease, high blood pressure, some kinds of cancer, and a myriad of other diseases, exercise can dramatically improve the quality of the life you live today. It allows you to connect with your physical body, while allowing your mind to take a bit of a break. Indeed many women with depression who exercise claim it is the one time in their day that they feel relief from their symptoms. Part of the reason is that certain brain chemicals called endorphins, known to dull pain and invoke mild euphoria, are released whenever the body feels pain, including during vigorous exercise, when the muscles begin to tire and "burn."

It is important to note, however, that exercise need not be demanding or elaborate to be effective. Moderate exercise—defined as thirty minutes of daily light activity (such as walking, gardening, housecleaning)—is almost as beneficial to one's health as a higher level of activities (such as jogging and aerobics). The important thing is to set realistic goals and to choose activities you enjoy. If you've been sedentary for a number of months or years, deciding to train for next month's marathon would be counterproductive, both physically (you're liable to hurt yourself) and emotionally (by setting yourself an impossible goal, you're sure to feel like a failure when you don't meet it). Instead start slowly. Take a walk around your neighborhood. Perform some stretching exercises on the floor while you watch the news or a favorite sitcom. Join a gym that has a pool, and enjoy the sensual pleasure of gliding through the cool water.

Establish an ease with your mind-body connection

Stress is a fact of life for people living in late-twentieth-century America, and it's a special burden for those of us who also suffer from depression. Although there is no way to avoid stress—in fact stress can act as an appropriate and energizing stimulus to activity—you can lessen its potentially damaging effects by learning to help your body and mind relax for certain periods of time each day.

We really have two goals when it comes to stress reduction. The short-term goal involves finding ways to alleviate feelings of anxiety when they occur or preventing them from taking hold at all. The long-term goal involves achieving a more permanent sense of balance and confidence in yourself and your goals. Without question, the short-term goals are easier to achieve. There are any number of ways to de-stress in the short term. They include, among others:

***Biofeedback*:** One of the most scientific ways of exploring and utilizing the mind-body connection, biofeedback was developed when studies showed that animals given rewards or punishments could control bodily functions once thought to be completely automatic. Physicians used those findings to design ways for humans to control unconscious functions through conscious thought.

Although there are several biofeedback methods, they all have three things in common: (1) They measure a physiological function (such as muscle tension or heart rate); (2) they convert this measurement to an understandable form (like a computer-generated graph or chart, a blinking light, mercury levels in a thermometer, etc.); and (3) they feed this information back to you.

If you have particular problems dealing with stress, talk to your therapist about biofeedback. It may help you feel the way your thought processes affect your body, and vice versa, in a more tangible way.

***Guided imagery*:** The human imagination—the part of our heart and mind that can picture and sense images and feelings—is one of the most potent health resources available to us. By utilizing the power of your mind, you can help evoke a physical and emotional response in order to relax your muscles, stimulate your immune system, and reduce your physical and emotional pain.

''My therapist suggested I think of my dark mood

as a cloud that I could push away," Dianne says. "She told me whenever I felt a bad spell coming on to close my eyes and picture myself blowing at that cloud until it disappeared. At first I resisted, but once I gave it a chance, I found it helped a lot. I imagine too that I can push away the Alzheimer's, that I can at least moderate its progress by picturing that cloud floating away. I know I'm in the earliest stages of this disease, and this might not work forever, but it's helping me now."

Although it is possible to conduct your own guided imagery session, it's best when learning to have a trained professional, preferably someone who has experience with treating people with depression, develop a program for you and guide you through the steps until they become familiar. Talk to your therapist if the idea interests you.

Meditation: Like biofeedback and guided imagery, meditation is a mental exercise that affects body processes. Meditation is performed for a host of reasons: religious, spiritual, and physical. When it comes to stress reduction, the purpose of meditation is to gain control over your thoughts so that you can focus on allowing the stress to flow out of your body. Meditation for relaxation requires no special training and can be done at any time of the day and in any comfortable space. All it takes is about fifteen minutes of uninterrupted quiet.

Meditation is effective in both reducing general stress and helping you relax your body and mind made tense by anxiety or worry. When you meditate, you quiet your nervous system, thereby reducing your heart rate and state of muscle contraction. Meditation can help you psychologically by allowing you to focus on the cause of your stress and to find ways to change the way you respond to the challenges you face. Researchers have found that when you meditate on a regular basis, you're able to come away with more positive feelings after a stressful encounter, sleep better, and tackle your challenges with more confidence.

"Meditation brought a sense of balance to my life," Janet says. "When I meditate, I close my eyes and imagine a round, soft pink ball in the pit of my stomach. This is my center. I see it there, weighing me down in a positive way, keeping me rooted in the here and now, but ready to move and sway and roll with whatever comes up. It really helps."

The relaxation response: One easy way to relax is to learn what is known as the "relaxation response." Developed in the 1970s by Herbert Benson, M.D., to counteract the fight or flight response during times of stress, the relaxation response works to bring the body back into balance quickly and efficiently. Here's a deep-breathing exercise that may help you trigger this relaxation response whenever you begin to feel over-stressed:

1. Sit on the floor in a comfortable position with your back straight and your head erect.
2. Close your eyes, and concentrate only on your breathing. Leave behind the worries of the day, and think only of this moment. Feel your breath as it flows into your mouth and nose and down into your lungs.
3. As you breathe in, picture your body filling with energy, light, and air. Feel your chest and your

upper back open up as air enters the area. The inhalation should take about five seconds.

4. When your lungs feel comfortably full, stop the movement and the intake of air. Exhale in a controlled, smooth continuous movement, the air streaming steadily out of your nostrils.

5. Repeat the inhalation-exhalations about four times a minute, resting about two or three seconds between breaths, until you feel better.

6. If you like, add a self-affirmation to your relaxation session by saying to yourself "I am in control. I am relaxed. I can manage my life," or some other positive thought every time you exhale.

Practice this relaxation technique as soon as you begin to feel overwhelmed by stress. You may find it especially helpful at work when trying to cope with the demands of your job might otherwise overwhelm and paralyze you.

"I can vouch for this one." Jake chuckles. "At first I felt like a fool when my doctor had me do it, but I was ready to try anything to stay well. And you know, it's true: If you're really concentrating on breathing, you don't have room in your brain for all the bad stuff. Now whenever I get upset or feel myself get all tense, I close my eyes and my mouth and breathe through my nose, these long, deep breaths. I feel better."

These simple relaxation methods, and others, can help you both cope with day-to-day stress-related challenges and imagine a path to longer-term peace and stability.

Avoiding Relapses

It would be pleasant to think that once you've beaten the monster of depression, you're rid of it forever. Unfortunately that's not always the case. Both Janet and her mother have fought lifelong battles with the disease, ultimately emerging victorious, but always staying alert to signs of its return. If you're just coming to terms with your own experience with depression, this may not be the time to worry about relapses. On the other hand, if you feel as if you've crossed the bridge to the other side, now's the time to start protecting yourself from relapses in the future. Here are some tips to get you started:

Find the right treatment: You may not find the right therapist on the first try, or your needs may change as you continue on your path of recovery. You may find your needs for medication change as well. Although energy and drive may be just what you lack at this time, it's vital that you keep at it until you find what works for you. Only with treatment will you reduce your risks of sinking deeper into depression or relapsing in just a few months' time.

Take your medication as prescribed: If you and your therapist decide you would benefit from an antidepressant or other medication, follow directions with care. Take the medication in the doses prescribed and for as long as your doctor recommends. Your instinct may be to stop taking the medication as soon as you feel better, but this would be a mistake. Studies have shown that patients are more likely to relapse if they stop taking medicine too soon. You'll probably want to take your medication for about six months to a year, but discuss the matter with your doctor.

Contact your doctor immediately if you start to feel depressed again: Watch for signs that depression may be returning. Are you starting to withdraw from your normal activities? Do you tire more easily than normal? Has your appetite changed? Are you more easily frustrated? Have you caught yourself crying at odd or inappropriate times? As soon as you feel you might be suffering a relapse, get into treatment. By doing so, you may be able to prevent another full-blown depressive episode from taking hold.

Take good care of your general health: Remember, mind and body are one and the same. Your brain and your spirit need the nutrients found in a good diet, the energy derived from healthy exercise, and the rejuvenation that comes with restful sleep and relaxation.

Reach out to others: You are not alone. If there's any message we hope you've received from this book loud and clear, it's that one. Not only are there people you know and love who can help you but there are millions of men and women who've traveled the very same dark road you've been on. Reach out to them, ask them for advice, learn from their experiences, and share your own with them.

Facing the Future with Optimism

Six months have now passed for the seven people you met at the beginning of the book. You've learned about some of the issues they've struggled with and have witnessed some of the progress they've made in conquering their disease. We hope their stories have helped you.

Today Nick feels as if he's "back to himself" again. At first resentful of his son's interference in his life, he's now thrilled to have the family together. "I get such a kick out of watching my granddaughter grow. She's only three, and it seems like she changes every day, learns something new, smiles in a different way," Nick says with a glow. "I missed that with my son because I worked so much. I think I'm most grateful to be well enough to enjoy this time with my family."

Working together with a therapist, Penny and her husband are exploring how the sexual abuse in her past affected their marriage in the past and in the present. They're learning to share their anxieties as well as their joys, something that these two people—once busy executives—never really knew how to do in their youth. "In a way my depression saved my life and my marriage," Penny explains. "I suppose we might have made it through to death without divorcing, but we would have grown farther and farther apart. Now we've got a chance to experience the coming years together, to learn from each other, to nurture each other. It's hard, but it's worth it."

Peter and his wife, Shannon, recently took a vacation together—all alone, away from their children and grandchildren—for the first time since their honeymoon twelve years ago. "Getting away was great, at least for me. I didn't realize how much the hubbub of family life had been wearing me out. I finally got to connect with my wife again and with myself and what I need at home. And I think we fell in love with each other again, just the two of us. It was good to know that she loves me not just because she loves the family we have together. And it was important for me to realize that I love her in the same way, despite our age difference.'' When Peter returned home, he entered analysis in order to continue the self-exploration his experience with depression triggered.

Janet now feels strong enough to consider what the best living situation for her mother and herself is likely to be in the future. ''We've been living together for more than ten years, ever since my husband left me,'' Janet says. ''And I don't think it's healthy anymore for either of us. She's eighty-three now and has medical needs I'm not really equipped to deal with—at least not if I want to have a life of my own. It's funny, I've been so afraid to talk to her about moving into an assisted-living situation that I've never even mentioned it. I was really surprised when it turned out she'd been thinking about it too. She wanted more contact with people her own age. She told me she'd been sticking around here for my sake! Now all we have to figure out is how to afford it—not easy, I'll tell you—but I think we'll manage it. Then I'm going to start really living again.''

''Loneliness. Loneliness and structure. That's what the doctor and I decided to tackle first,'' Jake says. ''I'm only sixty-eight. My life isn't over. I can do something more with my time and experience. So I'm volunteering at the Boys Club in the city. I've been working with the basketball team—whipping them into shape for the next season—and there's talk that the organization might want me to take over the whole athletic program when I'm ready. One day at a time, my therapist keeps telling me. But I like this challenge. I feel good again. And I know my daughter does too.'' What Jake doesn't offer is the news that he's met a woman through his volunteer work, a woman he's asked to dinner more than once. ''I'm thrilled for my dad,'' Julie says with a smile. ''At first it was strange that he'd begun to date—date! think of that!—but now I realize what a remarkable gift that is, to want to let your heart go free again.''

In addition to beginning to make some concrete plans about her future, Dianne has started keeping a journal, one she hopes she'll have the time and ability to turn into a magazine article, that chronicles her struggle with depression and Alzheimer's disease. '' 'Write about what you know' is the old adage, and so I'm going to give it a try. So far it's been good therapy for me, allowing me to talk through some of my own issues. But it's also given me an excuse—as if I needed one—to do more research about both conditions and to talk to other people like me who've dealt with the same kind of challenges. I've met some amazingly strong men and women, and I'm so grateful for their insight, not only for my work but for my soul.''

''Okay, I give in,'' Maude says with a laugh. ''Mike and his family are going to move upstairs as soon as that awful tenant is out of the house.'' Maude's son explains in more detail: ''Mom's never been one to admit she needs help, and compromise was certainly never her strong point. She wouldn't think of giving up the house or moving in with us, so we gave up and moved in with her. Luckily my kids are grown now, and my wife and I are kind of looking forward to moving into a smaller place. Both of us will feel better at being able to keep an eye on Mom.''

As you can see, depression is not an endless dark tunnel, nor does it represent a normal and inevitable side effect of aging. Instead it is a condition for which several very successful treatments are available. If you or someone you love struggles with depression today, please seek the needed help now so that the tomorrows can be as satisfying as possible.

In the Resource Guide on page 252 you'll find a list of organizations that can provide you with further information about depression and other mental disorders. These groups can refer you to qualified therapists and support groups in your area as well as send you pamphlets about the symptoms of depression, the medication and other therapies available to treat it, and the research into its causes and treatment being conducted in laboratories around the world.

Important Questions and Answers About Chapter 8

Q. I've experienced a number of losses lately. My husband and I moved into a new retirement community (leaving a family home of twenty-five years) two years ago, then he died suddenly about six months ago. I'm pretty much alone now, since my only sister died two years ago and my daughter lives in another state. I'm taking medication for a depression that set in a few months after my husband passed away, but now I feel ready to start making friends. But I don't know where to begin. Any suggestions?

A. One of the best things about retirement communities is that they usually provide lots of activities for their residents—activities that not only satisfy your interests but also introduce you to people who share those interests. It's much easier to start a conversation about golf with someone who also enjoys the game, for instance, and then to go to other topics and issues. (A game like golf, an exercise class, or walking group also provides some exercise, which will help you through your depression in another way as well!)

A note of caution: You may still be emotionally vulnerable, so it's important for you to take things slowly. It takes time—and a certain amount of luck—to find a friend and develop a lasting friendship. Try to meet a lot of different people and enjoy group activities; closer, more personal relationships will form naturally through that process.

Q. I'm a seventy-five-year-old woman who's suffered bouts of depression all my life, some of them pretty severe (there were two suicide attempts). I've been taking medication for the latest episode for about a year and feel pretty good now. My doctor is suggesting, though, that I stay on a low dose of this antidepressant pretty much indefinitely so I don't relapse. Could that be dangerous?

A. Without knowing your medical history, it's impossible to answer that question with absolute certainty but, in general, antidepressants are quite safe for most people even over many years. With your history of severe depression, your doctor may feel that the relatively small risks associated with antidepressants are well worth the benefits that come with maintaining your mental health. Talk to your doctor about your concerns. However, if you decide not to continue with drug therapy, remain alert to the signs of a relapse so that you can start treatment quickly in the future.

Q. I'm sixty-four years old, with a mild heart condition. I'm undergoing psychotherapy for depression, and am starting to feel better. My wife and I really enjoy having wine with our dinner, but I've heard that alcohol is a depressant. Should I avoid it altogether?

A. It is true that alcohol is a depressant and that drinking can only exacerbate your problems—especially if you use alcohol as a way to avoid facing your problems. On the other hand, a moderate amount of alcohol can indeed help you relax, add to the enjoyment of a meal, and even help reduce the risks of heart disease. Unless you're taking medication for depression or another ailment that prohibits alcohol, then, a glass of wine in the evenings may be perfectly all right for you to have. Talk to your doctor about it. Remember that finding balance and satisfaction in your life is the ultimate key to good emotional, physical, and mental health.

Glossary

Acetylcholine: A neurotransmitter that helps regulate memory. It also is one of the principal NEUROTRANSMITTERS involved in bodily functions that we think of as automatic, such as sweating and heart rate.

Addiction: A pattern of behavior based on a great physical and/or psychological need for a substance or activity. Addiction is characterized by compulsion, loss of control, and continued repetition of a behavior no matter what the consequences.

Alcoholism: Chronic and extreme physical dependence on alcohol characterized by tolerance to its effects and withdrawal symptoms when consumption is reduced or stopped. This disease involves complex cultural, social, and physical factors.

Anhedonia: The inability to experience pleasure and loss of interest in activities that once offered pleasure. A common symptom of depression.

Anorexia: A chronic, sometimes fatal eating disorder involving a loss of appetite or inability to eat that results in malnutrition, severe weight loss, and medical complications. (Anorexia nervosa, a distinct disorder, involves distortions in body image and perfectionism.) Anorexia is frequently associated with depression.

Antidepressants: Any of a number of drugs used to treat and relieve depression, including SELECTIVE SEROTONIN REUPTAKE INHIBITORS, TRICYCLIC ANTIDEPRESSANTS, and MONOAMINE OXIDASE INHIBITORS.

Antipsychotics: Any of a number of drugs used to treat the symptoms of psychosis, including hallucinations and delusions.

Anxiety: Uneasiness, worry, uncertainty, and fear that come with thinking about an anticipated danger. Anxiety may be a normal reaction to a real threat or occur when no danger exists.

Anxiety disorders: Any of several psychological disorders characterized by inappropriate and excessive physical and emotional symptoms of ANXIETY, such as restlessness, rapid heartbeat and respiration, and fear. PANIC DISORDER, OBSESSIVE-COMPULSIVE DISORDER, POSTTRAUMATIC STRESS DISORDER, and GENERALIZED ANXIETY DISORDER are the most common anxiety disorders. Anxiety disorders are frequently associated with depression.

Attention Deficit Disorder (ADD): A treatable neurobiological disorder characterized by symptoms of inattention, impulsivity and, often, hyperactivity, with an onset in childhood that causes significant impairment in school, work, or social adjustment.

Atypical depression: A form of major depression involving symptoms that include increased appetite, weight gain, and sleeping more than usual, often associated with heightened sensitivity to being rejected.

Behavioral therapy: A type of PSYCHOTHERAPY that attempts to change behavior by rewarding a desired behavior, punishing unwanted behavior, or withholding rewards for unwanted behaviors.

Benzodiazepines: Medications, including Valium and Librium carbonate, used to treat ANXIETY DISORDERS. At least one benzodiazepine, Xanax, has been shown to be possibly effective in treating depression.

Bipolar disorder: A mood disorder characterized by recurrent, alternating episodes of depression and MANIA. Formerly called manic depression.

Catecholamines: A group of structurally related NEUROTRANSMITTERS, including SEROTONIN, NOREPINEPHRINE, and DOPAMINE, thought to be involved in the pathology of depression and other emotional disorders.

Chronobiology: The study of internal body rhythms in order to map hormonal, nerve, and immune system cyclical functions. Some scientists believe that a disruption of normal body rhythms lies at the heart of depression.

Cognitive therapy: A therapeutic approach that considers depression the result of pessimistic ways of thinking and distorted attitudes about oneself and one's life. The patient is able to relieve depression by learning new ways to think about his or her situation through role playing, discussion, and assigned tasks.

Cortisol: One of the HORMONES produced by the body's adrenal glands, located above the kidneys. Cortisol is secreted in large amounts during times of stress and on a cyclical basis according to internal sleep and wake rhythms.

Cushing's disease: A disease in which the adrenal glands are overstimulated and thus produce an overabundance of the hormone CORTISOL. Symptoms of depression or mania may accompany the moonlike facial appearance, unusual fat deposits, and high blood pressure usually seen in this condition.

Delusion: A false belief held persistently despite abundant and clear evidence to the contrary.

Dementia: A cognitive disorder characterized by impaired memory, judgment, language, thinking, and perceptions.

Depression: A mental disorder that often involves feelings of sadness and despair, but also slowed thinking, decreased pleasure, appetite changes, sleeping difficulties, and/or physical aches and pains.

Dopamine: One of the CATECHOLAMINE NEUROTRANSMITTERS that may play a role in depression.

Dual diagnosis: The concurrent occurrence of a psychiatric disorder and a substance abuse disorder in the same individual at the time of diagnosis.

Dysthymia: A chronic depressive state that lasts at least two years with symptoms more mild (but longer-lasting) than major depression. Symptoms include feelings of inadequacy, hopelessness, low energy, and an inability to enjoy pleasurable activities.

Electroconvulsive therapy (ECT): The application of electric current to the brain through electrodes attached to the scalp. The electricity induces a convulsive seizure that often helps alleviate depression.

Endocrine system: The network of glands and tissues that produces HORMONES and secretes them into the blood for transport to target organs. Disorders of the endocrine system often cause depressive symptoms.

Endorphins: Chemicals that help to elevate mood and alleviate pain. Low levels of endorphins are related to depression.

Epinephrine: A substance produced by the adrenal gland, often in response to stress. Also called adrenaline, it is responsible for many of the physical manifestations of fear and anxiety.

Estrogen: The sex HORMONE that plays a major role in the development and maintenance of female secondary sex characteristics.

Family therapy: Therapy that focuses on understanding and improving marital partnerships and family relationships as a way to treat an individual's or a family's emotional or psychological problems.

Generalized anxiety disorder: An ANXIETY DISORDER characterized by unrealistic and excessive apprehension about life circumstances that lasts for more than six months and interferes with normal functioning.

Hormones: Substances secreted by the ENDOCRINE SYSTEM that have specific effects on other organs and processes. Hormones often are referred to as chemical messengers, and they influence such diverse activities as growth, sexual development, metabolism, and sleep cycles.

Huntington's chorea: An inherited and often fatal disease that causes affected individuals to lose their intellectual abilities and eventually become unable to control their movements. Symptoms of depression and/or bipolar disorder often appear early in the course of this condition.

Insomnia: A chronic inability to fall asleep, or to remain asleep, at night. A variety of factors, including diet and exercise habits, emotional stress, and hormonal imbalances, causes insomnia.

Interpersonal psychotherapy: A form of therapy that focuses on relationship issues in order to help individuals cope with depression by improving their interpersonal skills.

Learned helplessness: The passive acceptance of painful or disturbing stimuli after a period during which escape from the stimuli has been blocked. Learned helplessness has been proposed as a potential trigger for depression.

Lithium carbonate: A naturally occurring mineral salt used to treat BIPOLAR DISORDER.

Mania: The high phase of BIPOLAR DISORDER. Symptoms may include excessive elation, inflated self-esteem, hyperactivity, and rapid and confused speaking and thinking patterns.

Manic depression: See BIPOLAR DISORDER.

Marital therapy: Therapy intended to improve relationships between married partners.

Monoamine oxidase inhibitors (MAOIs): Antidepressant medication that works by inhibiting monoamine oxidase, an enzyme that breaks down NOREPINEPHRINE, SEROTONIN, DOPAMINE, and other NEUROTRANSMITTERS.

Mood disorders: A group of disorders characterized by disturbances in mood, including depression, BIPOLAR DISORDER, and conditions triggered by certain illnesses and medications.

Narcotic: Any drug that is derived from or has a chemical structure similar to that of an opiate and that relieves pain and alters mood. Most narcotics are addictive.

Neurons: Nerve cells; the basic units of the nervous system. Neurons are able to conduct impulses and communicate by releasing and receiving NEUROTRANSMITTERS.

Neurotransmitters: Chemicals that result in the sending of nerve signals, including SEROTONIN, DOPAMINE, and NOREPINEPHRINE. Neurotransmitters are released by NEURONS. When an imbalance occurs, emotional and physical symptoms often result.

Norepinephrine: A CATECHOLAMINE NEUROTRANSMITTER thought to be involved in affective disorders like depression.

Obsessive-compulsive disorder (OCD): An ANXIETY DISORDER characterized by recurrent obsessions or compulsions that impair the ability to function in daily life or form significant relationships. Depression often occurs with OCD.

Panic disorder: Recurrent attacks of panic that involve sudden, unprovoked intense fear or discomfort, usually lasting several minutes or longer. Physical symptoms can include rapid heartbeat, dizziness, nausea, shortness of breath, and feeling as if one is losing control.

Phobia: An unreasonable fear surrounding a specific object, activity, or situation. Phobias are frequently associated with ATYPICAL DEPRESSION.

Phototherapy: Treatment for depression in which the patient is exposed to bright lights for several hours each day. Phototherapy is particularly useful for sufferers of SEASONAL AFFECTIVE DISORDER.

Posttraumatic stress disorder (PTSD): An ANXIETY DISORDER occurring after exposure to extreme mental or physical stress—usually involving death, threatened death, or serious injury—and characterized by symptoms that persist for one month or more. Symptoms include reexperiencing the event, avoidance of stimuli related to it, and, frequently, an associated depression.

Psychiatrist: A licensed medical doctor who specializes in the diagnosis and treatment of mental and emotional disorders. A psychiatrist can prescribe medications.

Psychoanalysis: A form of therapy originally developed by Sigmund Freud that seeks to identify repressed issues and emotional conflicts from childhood. Techniques involve free association and dream interpretation. The process usually involves frequent sessions—often one hour every day—over a long period of time.

Psychodynamic psychotherapy: Therapy that focuses on the role of early experiences and unconscious influences on current behavior.

Psychologist: A person with a doctoral degree (Ph.D. or Psy.D.) in psychology that includes training in counseling, PSYCHOTHERAPY, and psychological testing.

Psychoneuroimmunology: The study of how the nervous system and immune system interact in the body.

Psychopathology: The study of the development, symptoms, and nature of mental disorders.

Psychopharmacology: The study of the actions and effects of drugs that work to alter emotions and behavior in people and animals.

Psychotherapy: Treatment for psychiatric disorders involving support, reassurance, and reeducation of the patient.

Psychotropic: A term used to describe the drugs used to treat mental and emotional illness.

Rapid cycling: A condition in BIPOLAR DISORDER in which four or more episodes of mood disturbance (mania, depression, or both) occur within a year or less.

Receptors: Specialized molecules on the surface of NEURONS to which particular NEUROTRANSMITTERS attach after their release from another neuron. This binding allows a message to be passed from one neuron to another.

Schizophrenia: A mental disorder characterized by such psychotic symptoms as delusions and hallucinations. The onset is generally between late adolescence and the mid-thirties.

Seasonal affective disorder (SAD): A type of depression that recurs at a particular time of year, usually during the fall and winter months, when daylight hours are shortest.

Selective serotonin reuptake inhibitor (SSRI): A type of ANTIDEPRESSANT that works to prevent the reuptake of the NEUROTRANSMITTER SEROTONIN. This increases the amount of serotonin in the spaces between neurons and allows messages about emotion and behavior to be sent and received more efficiently.

Self-esteem: A sense of self-worth and of valuing oneself as a person.

Serotonin: A NEUROTRANSMITTER found in the brain and the body that is involved in behavior, emotion, and appetite.

Side effect: An unintended drug response that accompanies the intended effect of a particular drug.

Stress: Anything that causes an action or reaction in the body, positive or negative, emotional or physical.

Stressor: Any factor—physical or emotional—that has an effect on the body.

Substance abuse: The compulsive use of alcohol or drugs despite the ill effects these substances cause to one's emotional, social, and physical well-being.

Suicide: The taking of one's life.

Synapse: The gap between the nerve endings of two NEURONS. For a message to pass across the synapse, it needs help from a NEUROTRANSMITTER.

Thyroid gland: An endocrine gland located in the neck.

Tricyclic antidepressants: Any of several ANTIDEPRESSANT drugs that have a three-ring chain as part of their chemical structure.

Tyramine: A chemical food in many foods that can cause a dangerous rise in blood pressure when a drug of the MONOAMINE OXIDASE INHIBITOR class is taken.

Unipolar depression: A mood disorder in which only episodes of depression occur. It is unlike BIPOLAR DISORDER, in which episodes of both MANIA and depression occur.

Resource Guide

The irony of depression is that it is at once a disease that iso-
lates and one that creates a "lasting fellowship" among its
sufferers, as William Styron phrases it in his memoir *Darkness Visible*. Although it may seem impossible to reach out of
your own personal darkness—even to grasp a helping hand—
that's one of the best forms of treatment around.

The associations listed below offer information, most of it free,
about different aspects of aging, depression, and other
chronic illnesses. In addition to their addresses and phone
numbers, we list (where applicable) their Internet addresses
(we even list an Internet resource for older people interested
in becoming more computer literate—see "SeniorNet," page
256). Please be advised that many Web pages offer links to
other sources of information but that not all these sources are
reputable. Make sure to talk to your doctor about any issue,
treatment, or theory that interests you, before you assume
that it has merit or is right for you. If you want to know more
about the disease, feel free to make use of these resources to
help educate yourself and your family.

Healthy Aging

American Association for Retired People
601 E Street NW
Washington, DC 20049
(202) 434-2277
On-line contact: http://www.aarp.org

  The AARP is a nonprofit organization dedicated to helping
  older Americans achieve lives of independence, dignity, and
  purpose.

Gray Panthers
2025 Pennsylvania Avenue, NW, Suite 141
Washington, DC 20006
(202) 466-3132

  Founded in 1970, the Gray Panthers is a multigenerational education and advocacy organization that works to bring about
  fundamental social changes, including a national health care
  system, elimination of all forms of discrimination, and eco-
  nomic justice. It publishes a newsletter and a newspaper and
  offers advice on how to create a local chapter. Annual dues
  are $20.

Alcohol and Substance Abuse

Alcoholics Anonymous World Services, Inc.
AA General Service Office
PO Box 459 Grand Central Station
New York, NY 10163
(212) 870-3400
Local branches nationwide: Check your local phone directory
On-line contact: http://www.alcoholics-anonymous.org

  Founded in 1935, Alcoholics Anonymous is a worldwide fellowship of men and women who have found a solution to
  their drinking problem. The only requirement for membership is a desire to stop drinking. AA is supported by the

voluntary contributions of its members and groups and neither seeks nor accepts outside funding. Members observe personal anonymity at the public level, thus emphasizing AA principles rather than personalities.

Al-Anon Family Groups, Inc.
1600 Corporate Landing Parkway
Virginia Beach, VA 23456
(804) 563-1600
(800) 344-2666
Local branches nationwide: Check your local phone directory
On-line contact: http://www.al-anon.org

Alzheimer's Disease

Alzheimer's Disease and Related Disorders
919 North Michigan Avenue, Suite 1000
Chicago, IL 60611
(800) 272-3900
On-line contact: http://www.alz.org

With 220 chapters and 1,600 support groups, the ADRD offers information and assistance for caregivers of Alzheimer's disease, including a newsletter, literature, and a chapter development kit so that you can start your own group in your neighborhood.

Caregiving

Children of Aging Parents (CAPS)
1609 Woodburne Road, Suite 302A
Levittown, PA 19057
(800) 227-7294

A national organization with thirteen local groups, CAPS is a nonprofit organization dedicated to the needs of the caregivers of the elderly, offering support and information, referrals, and counseling. CAPS publishes a bimonthly newsletters and offers brochures, books, and other materials at a low cost. It also offers assistance in starting new chapters.

National Family Caregivers Association
9621 East Bexhill Drive
Kensington, MD 20895
(301) 942-6430 or
(800) 896-3650
On-Line contact: http://www.ravens-nest.com/nfca
This nationwide network, founded in 1992, is dedicated to improving the quality of life for family caregivers. It offers its members a chance to network together for support and offers resources, literature, information, and referrals. Annual dues are $18.

Chronic Illness

American Diabetes Association
1660 Duke Street
Alexandria, VA 22314
(800) 232-3472
On-line contact: http://www.diabetes.org
ADA has fifty-one affiliates nationwide and seeks to improve the well-being of people with diabetes and their families. Annual dues of $24 include a monthly magazine.

Arthritis Foundation
PO Box 7669
Atlanta, GA 30357
(800) 283-7800
The Arthritis Foundation has sixty-five chapters nationwide offering education, support, and activities for people with arthritis and their families and friends. It also provides self-help instruction programs and a bimonthly magazine.

Stroke Connection of the American Heart Association
7272 Greenville Avenue
Dallas, TX 75231
(800) 553-6321
On-line contact: http://www.amhrt.org

> With a thousand groups nationwide, the Stroke Connection maintains a listing for stroke survivors, their families, caregivers, and interested professionals. It publishes a Stroke Connection magazine, which is a forum for stroke survivors and their families to share information about coping with strokes, as well as offers stroke-related books, videos, and literature for sale.

Computer Literacy

On-line contact: http://www.seniornet.com

> This is an international community of computer-using seniors. The Web page offers basic information and instruction about computer technologies to adults fifty-five and older.

Eating Disorders

American Anorexia/Bulimia Association, Inc.
293 Central Park West, Suite 1R
New York, NY 10024
(212) 501-8351

> The association offers information in the form of brochures and videotapes about eating disorders as well as provides referrals to clinics, therapists, hospital programs, and support groups. Specify that you're interested in understanding more about older people and anorexia if you request information.

National Association of Anorexia Nervosa and Associated Disorders
Box 7

Highland Park, IL 60035
(847) 831-3438

> This organization operates a phone line from 9:00 A.M. to 5:00 P.M. providing free information, telephone counseling, and nationwide referrals to therapists, support groups, and physicians who specialize in eating disorders.

Mental Health

American Psychiatric Association
1400 K Street NW
Washington, DC 20005
(202) 682-6220

American Psychological Association
750 First Street NE
Washington, DC 20002
(202) 336-5500

Anxiety Disorders Association of America
6000 Executive Boulevard, Department A
Rockville, MD 20852
(301) 231-9350
On-line contact: http://www.adaa.org

> A national network of consumers, health care professionals, and other concerned individuals, the ADAA offers a national membership directory, a self-help-group directory, and a newsletter.

Depression Awareness, Recognition, and Treatment (D/ART)
Program Department GL
Room 10-855600 Fishers Lane
Rockville, MD 20857
(800) 421-4211

> D/ART is a federally funded project created by the National

Institutes of Health providing free brochures and booklets about all aspects of depression.

National Alliance for the Mentally Ill (NAMI)
2101 Wilson Boulevard, Suite 302
Arlington, VA 22201
(703) 524-7600
On-line contact: http://www.nami.org
  Founded in 1972 as a grass roots self-help, support, and advocacy organization, NAMI now includes more than a thousand affiliated groups operating in all fifty states. It provides free information on psychiatric illnesses, medicines, and financial concerns related to mental health care.

National Depressive and Manic Depressive Association
53 West Jackson Boulevard, Room 618
Chicago, IL 60604
(800) 82-NDMDA
On-line contact: http://www.ndmda.org
  This organization with 265 local chapters offers free brochures about depression and bipolar disorders as well as information about support groups. It provides public education on the biochemical nature of depressive illness with annual conferences, advice on chapter development, and a bookstore and catalog. Membership in NDMDA ($20 per year) entitles you to a quarterly newsletter.

National Foundation for Depressive Illness
PO Box 2257
New York, NY 10016
(212) 268-4260
  The National Foundation for Depressive Illness offers referrals to specialists in mood disorders as well as an extensive bibliography of books about depression and bipolar disorder.

National Institute of Mental Health
Public Inquiries, Room 7C-02
5600 Fishers Lane
Rockville, MD 20857
On-line contact: http://www.nimh.nih.gov

National Mental Health Association (NMHA)
National Mental Health Information Center
1021 Prince Street
Alexandria, VA 23314-2971
(800) 969-6642

Books

Reading about the experiences of therapists, researchers, and, above all, other people who suffer with depression can be both comforting and illuminating. So too can learning the good and bad news about all aspects of the aging process. Go to your local library or bookstore to see if any of the titles listed below pique your interest.

Barlow, David H. *Anxiety and Its Disorders*. New York: Guilford, 1988.

Beck, Aaron T. *Love Is Never Enough*. New York: Harper & Row, 1988.

Berg, Robert L., and Joseph S. Cassels, eds. *The Second Fifty Years: Promoting Health and Preventing Disability*. Institute of Medicine. Washington, D.C.: National Academy Press, 1990.

Berger, Diane and Lisa. *We Heard the Angels of Madness: How One Family Dealt with Manic Depression*. New York: William Morrow, 1991.

Bloomfield, Harold H., M.D., and Peter McWilliams. *How to Heal Depression*. Los Angeles: Prelude Press, 1994.

Braiker, Harriet. *Getting Up When You're Feeling Down: A*

Woman's Guide to Overcoming and Preventing Depression. New York: Putnam, 1988.

Butler, Robert M., and Myrna I. Lewis. *Love and Sex After Sixty.* New York: Harper & Row, 1988.

Chan, Connie S. *Depression: Reducing Your Risk (If It Runs in Your Family).* New York: Bantam Books, 1993.

Cleve, Say, Ph.D. *Out of the Blues.* New York: Berkeley Books, 1989.

Cohen, David. *Out of the Blue: Depression and Human Nature.* New York: W. W. Norton, 1994.

Cronkite, Kathy. *On the Edge of Darkness: Conversations About Conquering Depression.* New York: Doubleday, 1994.

DePaulo, J. Raymond, Jr., and Keith Russell Ablow. *How to Cope with Depression: A Complete Guide for You and Your Family.* New York: McGraw-Hill, 1989.

Dowling, Colette. *You Mean I Don't Have to Feel This Way?* New York: Scribners, 1991.

Dukakis, Kitty. *Now You Know.* New York: Simon & Schuster, 1990.

Duke, Patty, and Gloria Hochman. *A Brilliant Madness: Living with Manic-Depressive Illness.* New York: Bantam Books, 1992.

Engler, Jack, and Daniel Goldman. *The Consumer's Guide to Psychotherapy.* New York: Fireside, 1992.

Erikson, Erik H., Joan M. Erikson, and Helen Q. Kivnick. *Vital Involvement in Old Age: The Experience of Old Age in Our Time.* New York: W. W. Norton, 1986.

Fieve, Ronald R. *Prozac: Questions and Answers for Patients, Family, and Physicians.* New York: Avon, 1994.

Friedan, Betty. *The Fountain of Age.* New York: Simon & Schuster, 1993.

Goldberg, Ivan K., M.D. *Questions and Answers About Depression and Its Treatment: A Consultation with a Leading Psychiatrist.* Philadelphia: Charles Press, 1993.

Goodwin, F. K., and K. R. Jamison. *Manic-Depressive Illness.* New York: Oxford University Press, 1990.

Hauri, Peter, Ph.D., and Shirley Linde, Ph.D. *No More Sleepless Nights.* New York: John Wiley & Sons, 1991.

Hendin, Herbert, M.D. *Suicide in America.* New York: W. W. Norton, 1995.

Hirschfeld, Robert. *When the Blues Won't Go Away.* New York: Macmillan, 1991.

Ingersoll, Barbara D., Ph.D., and Sam Goldstein, Ph.D. *Lonely, Sad, and Angry: A Parent's Guide to Depression in Children and Adolescents.* New York: Doubleday, 1995.

Jamison, Kay Redfield, M.D. *An Unquiet Mind: A Memoir of Moods and Madness.* New York: Knopf, 1995.

Klein, Donald F., and Paul H. Wender. *Understanding Depression.* New York: Oxford University Press, 1993.

Kramer, Peter D. *Listening to Prozac.* New York: Viking, 1993.

Mace, Nancy L., and Peter V. Rabins. *The 36-Hour Day: A Family Guide to Caring for Persons with Alzheimer's Disease, Related Dementing Illnesses, and Memory Loss in Later Life.* Baltimore: Johns Hopkins University Press, 1991.

McGrath, Ellen, et al., eds. *Women and Depression.* Washington, D.C.: American Psychological Association, 1990.

Oster, Gerald, D., Ph.D., and Sarah S. Montgomery, M.S.W. *Helping Your Depressed Teenager: A Guide for Parents and Caregivers.* New York: John Wiley & Sons, 1995.

Papolos, Demitri F., and Janice Papolos. *Overcoming Depression.* New York: Harper & Row, 1997.

Real, Terrence. *I Don't Want to Talk About It.* New York: Scribners, 1997.

Rosenthal, Norman E. *Winter Blues.* New York: Guilford, 1993.

Salmans, Sandra. *Depression: Questions You Have . . . Answers You Need.* Allentown, Pa.: People's Medical Society, 1995.

Sheehy, Gail. *Passages.* New York: E. P. Dutton, 1976.

———. *New Passages.* New York: Random House, 1995.

Silverstone, Barbara, and Helen Kandel Hyman. *Growing Older*

Together: A Couple's Understanding and Coping with the Challenges of Later Life. New York: Random House, 1992. *You and Your Aging Parent.* New York: Random House, 1989.

Styron, William. *Darkness Visible: A Memoir of Madness.* New York: Random House, 1990.

Thompson, Tracy. *The Beast: A Reckoning with Depression.* New York: Putnam, 1995.

Wurtzel, Elizabeth. *Prozac Nation: Young and Depressed in America.* New York: Houghton Mifflin, 1994.

Index